THE BEGINNERS GUIDE TO THE TAI CHI FORM

PAUL READ

CRAVING
distraction
#Limited

The Beginners Guide to the Tai Chi Form

ISBN: 9781804676561
Perfect Bound

First published 2010
2025 Edition by Bookvault Publishing, Peterborough, United Kingdom
An environmentally friendly book printed and bound in England, powered by
printondemand-worldwide

CONTENTS

SECTION I: BEGINNINGS

"If the lessons of history teach us anything it is that nobody learns the lessons that history teaches us."

A WORD OR TWO

A word or two about learning Tai Chi

It is a sad fact that in many Tai Chi schools, the majority of students dropout before finishing their course. Teachers, when asked, explain that students lack the patience and commitment to learn. Students, however, point out that there are other reasons.

Learning Tai Chi is not so easy, for the postures are complex, require a level of coordination and balance skills rarely seen outside the juggling or tight-rope walking professions, and require a dedication to a long-term learning program that may take years to grasp even the basics.

Students also pointed out three additional areas of concern:

1. For a number of reasons, they are not always motivated to practice every day of their lives.
2. That work, family, and social pressure infringe on free

time, so they need a Form that can adapt to the time available.

3. Not everyone has a training hall at home, so any Tai Chi Form should also be able to adapt to the space available.

Consequently, I began to put together a more flexible Tai Chi Form that would be easier and quicker to learn and one that would act as a good basis for further studies.

I looked into the history of the art to see if there were examples I could use. To my surprise, I discovered that most schools and most teachers had (consciously or unconsciously) adapted and amended their respective Tai Chi Forms[1] when they were passed down from generation to generation.

Once I realised that this was an ongoing process, albeit an unspoken one, I started to assemble a new mini-set of postures that could be taught in just a few hours, yet, for students that wanted to learn more, it would also provide expandability and depth. To ensure that the postures would adhere to the basic principles of the art, I consulted the formative texts and have attempted to stay within the accepted guidelines.

Working through the book

This book follows a simple question-and-answer format wherever possible, offering bite-sized chunks of detail or instruction that can be better remembered. Feel free to jump around following a pattern that appeals to you. Although the pages follow a linear and numerical order, you may wish to create your own path through the chapters.

- Sections 1 and 2 look at the curious history of the Tai Chi Form and the resources I have used to build this particular set of postures.

- Section 3 is the one not to skip, for it lays the foundations of the moves that follow in sections 4 and 5.

- Section 6 is for all those who complete the Form and are looking for further challenges. Here you will find all the various ways to expand the number of moves, mirror the Form and adapt it further still.

- Section 7 provides all the references and resources you need for the moves you will learn in this book, as well as additional training to take your Tai Chi to the next level.

Visual aids and the limits of photography

Although this book, with its many photos and references, has been designed as a stand alone instruction manual, static images and text alone cannot do full justice to the Form and the moves. In fact, I'd go further and say that any static images are inherently limited in what they can offer. So I encourage you to focus on the description. The purpose of the images are to give a feel for each move, rather than a geometric angular account. For a more complete look, consult the Additional Resource section, where you will find video links to see the moves performed, additional images, audio files, and articles to help back up your Tai Chi practice.

The Online Version

For those that purchased the book from the Tai Chi Bookstore (see Chapt. 34), you will have received a code giving you free access to the online course. The course offers a moving demonstration of each exercise, each posture for greater detail and analysis. Feel free to jump back and forth, from chapter to online course as you work through the book.

Limits and focus

Tai Chi is a broad area of study, from martial applications and philosophy, to qigong, energy work, coordination, balance, posture, partner work, history, weapons, and the moves of the Form.

Were this book to try and cover all aspects of the art, it would be 1000's of pages in length and as such, be off-putting to anyone but the most obsessive of practitioners. And the art already has its fair share of these. So, instead, it aims to do just one thing, but to do it well: teach you a short sequence of Tai Chi moves that you can practice anywhere, anytime, for the rest of your life.

After this, should you need help or advice for your Tai Chi journey, feel free to contact me, using the links at the back of this book.

Peace and warm wishes,

Paul Read (teapotmOnk)

---

1. See Douglas Wiles excellent book on Yang Family Secret Transmissions for more on this subject, or listen to any of Professor Paul Bowman's podcast on Tai Chi's ancestry and lineage as it moved from east to west.

A QUICK Q&A ON TAI CHI FORMS

What is the Tai Chi Form?

When anyone thinks of learning Tai Chi, they generally think of the flowing, harmonious sequence of postures called the **Form**. These varied Forms are not exclusive to Tai Chi; though the emphasis, pace, and attention to body synchronisation are more focused, similar Forms do exist in all martial arts. In the Japanese arts of Karate, Kendo, Judo, and Aikido, for instance, the sequences of pre-ordered moves are called **kata**. In the Chinese arts, they are called **Forms**, and irrespective of the martial art you practice, many of the postures, moves, and stances are repeated between them all.

What is the difference between an internal and an external style?

Martial artists do like to define and categorise things, so they have created styles and sub-styles within their arts, each with their respective variations. This emphasis on categorisation can get very confusing, so to try and make some sense of it all, they label their arts according to country of origin: Japanese, Chinese, Korean, etc. This, however, was not enough, so they then placed all the arts into one of two camps: **external** and **internal**. What is meant by these is a little vague, but generally, some arts like to think they emphasise muscular force, power, and speed, while others concentrate on internal energy, posture, and breath. The reality is that both categories are very loose, and most schools will draw on all sources of energy and strength — muscular and tensile, straight and circular, fast and slow. Additionally, all arts emphasise the importance of breath, posture, coordination, etc.

However, despite this shared heritage and practice, Tai Chi is still seen as "different" by other martial artists, and often this difference is reflected in the practice of the Tai Chi Form, whether it be called a **long** or **short** Form, an **old** or **new** one, **large** or **small** frame. In general, all Tai Chi schools will teach beginners a single empty-handed Form for their first few years, while a karate practitioner, for example, may learn half a dozen **kata** during the same time-period.

Why such a different approach?

Tai Chi schools like to do things slowly. Generally, this is a good thing, but a potential issue arises if we obsess over the detail that becomes observable when we move at slow speeds. These details become points of debate as one style argues the merits of one interpretation over another. All martial arts fall prey to this to some extent, but only in Tai Chi is there a detailed and critical observation of not only the moves themselves but the transitions between moves too. Hence, it takes a lot longer to learn a Tai Chi Form than a similar length Form in another art.

Is the Form different in each of the styles?

There are a set of guidelines and general rules of movement that have been laid down over the years in a series of texts called the **Tai Chi Classics**, and each teacher will use these references to try to ensure their art remains faithful to its origins. Unfortunately, the guidelines are somewhat vague and open to interpretation, which may go some way to explaining the many variations between the different styles today. Among the main half-dozen styles of Tai Chi Chuan practised throughout the world, there exists over 120 different Tai Chi Forms each with their own number of moves ranging from 4 to over 200.

Over 200?

The number of variations in themselves does not present a problem, but when they are accompanied by claims of exclusive lineage, authenticity, and superiority of application, they present a confusing scenario for the new student looking for a simple pathway into the art. There was, and still remains a need for a simpler approach for anyone starting out on their Tai Chi journey. This book, therefore, has one simple aim: to gather together 10—12 postures common to all styles and teach them in such a way that they will be easy to learn in a very short time. Irrespective of the style you study today or will study tomorrow, these 10—12 postures will prove a good grounding for your training in Tai Chi.

Can you change or create a Form?

Many teachers would shake their heads in horror and say loudly and categorically, 'No!' Yet, when we look at the history of the Tai Chi Form, we see how it has changed and continues to change in all parts of the world. If we look at one of the most closely traced lineage systems—that of the Chen style, for instance—we can see that even here, the teaching of the Form has changed over time, introducing different lengths, variations, and what it describes as **frames**. And the universally popular Yang style appears to have undertaken an unbroken path of adaptation and evolution since its onset. See the following two chapters for a more detailed look at this history.

How am I going to learn the postures in this book?

I'm going to make it really easy for you by first showing you the basics of footwork and arm moves before you even start with the postures. Once you have practised these, you will take that knowledge into the sequence of postures. Finally, once you have worked through the basic 10-12 moves[1], I'll be explaining how to expand or contract your Form depending on the time, space, and energy you have available to practice.

And, at any time you want greater clarification, you can consult the online examples for moving demonstrations of each posture, transition, extension or exercise.

How is it possible to learn a Form this quickly?

There are several reasons why you can learn these postures fairly quickly. The first is that we are only going to start with 10 moves, not the hundreds that some other styles will teach. The second is that when attending local classes, it's unlikely you'll be able to work at your own pace. Normally, classes defer to the pace of the teacher, the fastest student, or the slowest student in the class, but it is not possible to work at the pace of 15 different students at the same time in the same class. If you do not work at your own pace, you will always feel that you are learning too fast or too slowly. Inevitably, if this is not tailored to your needs somehow, you may well end up dropping the class.

Another reason that you'll progress more quickly is that you'll learn according to your own preferences. Some students will learn better after seeing the moves repeated a hundred times, others just once. Some students need to hear a full description of each move; others need to only watch. Some will need to test out a single move many times before moving on; others will be happy learning three moves in one session. Teachers must always compromise in a class to find a midpoint and a general pace to satisfy everyone, irrespective of individual learning preferences.[2]

Why does this Form only have 10–12 moves?

Although it starts with 10, it then adds an optional beginning and end, making 12. Later, when you are confident with these first moves, I will show you how to expand the Form to 30, 40, or more moves. But I would rather focus on the essence of Tai Chi than get caught up in a discussion on numbers.

Will I need anything more than this book to learn the Form?

No. Everything is here. You will learn the basic footwork, arm moves and all 10 postures of this Form. If you want to learn more and there is a local class you can attend, then you'll find the background practice here useful in your future studies with other teachers. For clarification, you can consult the videos and resources at the end of this book. Remember, there is a video walk-through of every aspect of this book, including exercises, patterns, histories, etc. See the back of this book for more information about the free companion online resource.

Can we start now?

Hang on a moment! Before we throw ourselves straight into the physical training for Tai Chi footwork and positions, it is worth spending a few minutes to see what advice for learning the great masters of old left us and to look back over how the Tai Chi Form has arrived here. You see, there is a popular myth that the Forms of Tai Chi are untouchable — that we should never tamper with, change a single move or rearrange any of the postures. Yet the history of the art shows us something altogether different.

What if I am not interested in the history or the advice of the great masters of the past?

In that case, feel free to skip ahead to Section III. But don't say I didn't warn you...

---

1. The term "posture" or "move" is used to mean the defined moves/postures that make up a "Form" such as Play Guitar, or Brush Knee and Push. Occasionally the word, "move" is preferred by some schools as it denotes a transition as opposed to a fixed and held "posture". But at this point we demonstrate to the rest of the world that again we have degenerated into the realms of pedantry, so expect in this book to find both used indiscriminately throughout.
2. Take a look at the reference section for a link to the Tai Chi Illustrated Workbook - that will help you determine the way you learn best in a class.

2

A BRIEF HISTORY OF THE TAI CHI FORM

Our Tai Chi journey is a rather turbulent and troubled voyage, for in the not too distant past there was no social media to record the minutiae of everyday life. People created things, started movements, and overturned countries without the use of a mobile phone. Before Gutenberg and the later appearance of eBook readers, the unfolding of world events was passed down from generation to generation via oral accounts in the form of stories. These stories tell of the Tai Chi Form being created around the year 1200 by a legendary figure named **Chang San Feng**.

Chang San Feng was a Taoist priest who lived on the Wu Dan Mountain. It is said that one day he observed a fight between a mongoose and a snake. The fluid movements of the animals

inspired him to fuse the postures he had been practising separately into a single, flowing Form. San Feng continued to work on his Tai Chi Form until he was finally recognised for his achievements and granted immortality by the Taoist Immortals, who lived happily together in what was referred to as the Pink Palace in the Sky. Upon receiving the news, San Feng flew up to receive his award on the back of a White Crane (then the only transport that could carry him away to the Pink Palace), and there he lived happily ever after as a Taoist Immortal.

Hmm. Is there another version?

There is in fact another version of this history, though sadly there are no Pink Palaces, Immortals or Mongooses in this story. Instead, we must start at the Chen village in the Henan province of China around the seventeenth century. Here, like in many places across China, martial arts were practised by 'families' and each family had its own specific local or regional characteristics. The Chen villagers practiced a Form that combined a system of self-defence, influenced by, the nearby Shaolin temple. (Yes, that's right, the very same one that Kwai Chang Caine fled from in the 1970s TV series - *Kung Fu*.) This gradual development of the art continued for some time without anything very exciting happening, until, upon the scene, stepped an outsider called Yang Lu Chan (1799 - 1872).

Why is that name familiar?

Do remember that a mere hundred surnames still make up over 85% of China's 1.4 billion citizens, so it is not surprising that a few of these names will be familiar to you. The Yang name features heavily in the history of the art, as the Yang Tai Chi style is probably the most widely practised throughout the world today, and that is all down to Mr Yang. It is said that he spent a period of 18 years studying with the Chens, and, as is so often the case when an outsider strolls into an environment that has encountered little change over the years, things got stirred up. We don't know why other outsiders didn't do the same thing, or if they did, the stories are not told as often as this one. All we know is that the original system of Tai Chi stayed with the Chens until Yang learned the art. Eventually he moved out of the village and took his knowledge and skills to Beijing, where, presumably, fame and fortune called. There, he not only promoted the art of Tai Chi but also became the trainer for the Imperial Guard at the Forbidden Palace. He even had the audacity to rename the art, thereafter referring to it as the Yang style of Tai Chi.

Couldn't the Chens have copyrighted the name?

Possibly, but in those days it was more usual to take what was lying around and convert it into something else. All styles were created in this way, and as the famous Catalan architect Gaudí once said: '*Nothing is invented, for it is written in nature first.*'

Did the Chens take this lying down?

It is doubtful that the village celebrated the spread of their art under another person's name. Most likely, the head teachers looked aghast at what had happened to their long-preserved style. They argued amongst themselves about what to do. Yang had not only stolen their intellectual property but perverted its essence until it was no longer the same recognisable Tai Chi Form. Confused and divided, the Chens responded by making changes themselves, but these only resulted in further dividing and confusing their students. They turned their Tai Chi Forms into frame sets (based on the width of stances) and created Old or New frames, in reference to either the old tradition or the new tradition.

What? Now I am confused!

Don't worry; it's not just you. Let's leave the Chens and look for some clarity in Beijing, where Mr. Yang has been spreading his version of Tai Chi (Version 2.0) far and wide. Such was his success that one of his students, a man named Wu, began to create his own style of Tai Chi, called, somewhat predictably, Wu style. Karma had worked its magic on the man who took the Chen style Form and created his own. Now it had happened to him. In fact, it was happening everywhere. Suddenly, people were adapting, changing, and naming styles willy-nilly. Even within Mr. Yang's own family, Yang Chen Fu[1] (one of his grandchildren) set off to travel throughout China, teaching his grandfather's style but adapting and modifying it as he went.

The first known "Steam Punk Tai Chi Crew" with
Yang Chen Fu (and his cool hat)

Why would Yang change the Form?

As Yang Chen Fu moved from city to city, he would set himself up as a teacher and wait to see who would enrol in his classes. He noticed that in different places, people wanted to learn the art for different reasons. Not everyone joined his classes in order to learn how to defend their town against a warring overlord. Not everyone wanted to develop enough power to strike a mongoose dead at 50 yards with a secret mystical energy ray. Many turned up simply out of curiosity or because they just wanted to get healthy. To the martial arts purists, Yang Chen Fu had sold out, diluting the art and offering it up for consumption to people who were not prepared to give their lives to the legacy of the arts. Others, however, saw him as a visionary and credited his changes with enabling Tai Chi to survive healthily into the twenty-first century.

Meanwhile, just to keep the ball rolling, one of Yang Chen Fu's students, Cheng Man Ching, decided to remove a lot of the repetitions in the Yang Chen Fu Form, add some new rhythms of his

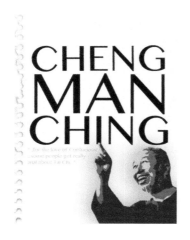

own, add some new transitions, and, to top it all off, rearrange the order of the postures. The Yang Chen Fu faithful stood aghast as Cheng Man Ching not only created a new shorter version of Yang Chen Fu's Form (made up of just 37 postures), but he then exported the whole thing to the West in the 1960s and began to do the one thing everyone had sworn not to do: teach foreigners.

Why did he go west?

In the middle of the twentieth century, many Chinese nobles aligned with opposition forces against Mao's Red Army. As the forces of revolution spread across the country, these families fled to settle in other countries—Australia, Taiwan, Malaysia, and later the US and Europe. This was a pattern that would repeat itself during the Cultural Revolution in the 1960s. Thus, Cheng Man Ching, for example, left China in 1949 for Taiwan before he was later invited to teach in the US. But there were others who migrated even before the revolution. The earliest recorded instance of Tai Chi being taken to the West was in 1939. And it was not just the Chinese demonstrating the art to Westerners. In 1954, Sophia Delza performed the first Tai Chi demonstration at the Museum of Modern Art. Cheng Man Ching and the rest of the political refugees were just following the paths of others before them. Despite his changes and his new Form not being officially recognised by the Yang family, Cheng Man Ching (and later his students) went on to spread the practice of Tai Chi across the whole of the Western world.*

Does our story end here?

Some stories never end, and the Tai Chi story still has a lot to play out. Immediately after Cheng Man Ching's death in the 1970s, several of his students decided to put back some of what their teacher had removed from the Form. And that process continues to this day.

What about all those people still teaching the original Yang Lu Chan Form?

It is true that some styles claim to authentically reproduce the exact same postures and moves as their founders taught. However, despite their best intentions, teachers do have a tendency to add things and take others out, sometimes without realising it them-selves. They often believe they remain faithful to the original, but unless you are still teaching in Mandarin, in Mainland China, in the 18th century, there will always be some conditions that are difficult to replicate.

Additionally, personality, character, physical health, shape, size, environment, fitness, and energy levels all contribute to the way a Form is taught, and that is as it should be if the art is to evolve and remain relevant to each new era.

Read more on how and why the young men and women of Tai Chi went west in this article.

---

1. When you finish this chapter and would like to know more about Yang Chen Fu's contributions to Tai Chi classics, watch the YouTube musical adaptation of his 10 principles listed in the resources section

3

LEARNING FROM HISTORY

"*I am not tempted* **TO BE THRUST BACK INTO MOCK ANTIQUITY**. *i prefer to strengthen – to adapt an art* **SO IT MAY BE OF USE IN OUR TIME**"

What can we learn from this history?

If we have learned anything from that rather mixed-up and crazy history of Tai Chi, it's that there is no such thing as a fixed, static, and unchangeable Tai Chi Form. It adapts, it changes, and it evolves wherever it goes and with whomever practises it, as Yang

Chen Fu discovered as he travelled through China, teaching modifications of his grandfather's Form.

Is there a consensus on how many moves should be in a Tai Chi Form?

Not really. What we call Long Forms tend to have (not surprisingly) more postures, while the Short Forms have fewer. Remember that there are over 100 variations of the Tai Chi Form and of these:

- 6 have 10 or fewer moves
- 18 have between 10 and 20 moves
- 7 have between 20 and 30 moves
- 19 have between 30 and 50 moves
- 24 have between 50 and 100 moves
- 11 have over 100 moves
- 1 has over 200 moves

With so many variations, how can anyone be sure that what they learn is correct?

This question is of such importance that it deserves a section in its own right, as the answer lies in a set of basic guidelines called the **Tai Chi Classics**.

SECTION II: HOW TO LEARN THE TAI CHI FORM

"Those are my principles. If you don't like them I have others."

GROUCHO MARX

INTRODUCTION TO SECTION II

In this section

I am going to introduce you to some of the fundamental writings on Tai Chi and try to answer the most common questions about the different styles, what is meant by lineage and authenticity, and even the importance (or not) of the colour of your belt.

4

ADVICE FROM THE WISE (OR NOT SO WISE)

HISTORY
PART 2

How do we know what we are doing is right?

We don't. Partly because almost every stage in the history of the martial arts has been hotly disputed and remains so, and partly because what was right for one country at a particular time in its history does not necessarily make it right for another population in another country at another time. In the martial arts, after all, it is in our training to recognise and respond to disputes and challenges given half a chance. In an art such as Tai Chi—an art that is heavily structured and yet amorphous at the same time—debates arise endlessly as to the meaning, purpose, and significance of each move. But let's not be deterred by this state of affairs.

Can I tell skill level by the colour of my instructor's belt?

Unlike the Japanese systems that have their familiar hierarchical structures of training, Tai Chi doesn't award coloured belts or gradings in recognition of skills.

What about hair cuts or silk suits?

See article on Gifts for Tai Chi Gurus in Additional Resources

Most Tai Chi teachers do not have certificates on walls, nor do they wear special clothing or adopt sumo-like topknots, though there is a tendency amongst some Westerners to grow a ponytail and wear a Chinese silk suit in the hope that this, in itself, confers wisdom and ancient knowledge. However, these outward displays often distract from the art's simplicity and its deeper, practical insights.

Can I tell by looking at the lineage or style?

Those who depend on such things would, of course, argue that you could. But lineage may not necessarily tell you as much as you hope. It all depends on why you are learning: do you wish to replicate an art as it was practised several centuries ago, or do you wish to learn an art relevant to the century in which you live?

Once upon a time, before the invention of the printing press, techniques and skills were handed down orally from master to student — hence Yang Lu Chan having to hike over to the Chen village to learn what they were doing. Therefore, the relationship between master and student (lineage) was crucial, as there were no other ways to learn what someone taught.

But later, when people began writing and disseminating instructions through books, lineage became less important. The question was no longer 'Do you have the information direct from the horse's mouth?' but rather, given that everyone can access this information relatively easily, 'Can you teach it effectively to another person and in a way that makes sense to them?

Then how can I tell?

It's not easy. Most of us agree on the usefulness of a set of guidelines on the principles of Tai Chi penned over the years by a number of writers and called the Tai Chi Classics. However, although they contain the basic guidelines for Tai Chi practitioners, they tend to be somewhat obtuse for a 21st-century Tai Chi player. Given such ambiguity in the Classics, I've extracted a few examples of the more important guidelines to assist you before we learn our Tai Chi Form. I'll list just a few here, but my advice is not to try and analyse them too much or even spend time trying to understand their depth of meaning. Instead, I suggest you just nod as though you understand and then come back to this chapter at a later point. Once you have worked on some of the postures and tried applying some of the principles of movement there, I'm sure they will make more sense to you.

5

ADVICE FROM THE PAST

The Tai Chi Classics are a collection of writings attributed (not always accurately) to a series of Tai Chi practitioners over the history of the art. We start with the legendary founder of Tai Chi whom you may remember from our dubious history section back in chapter 3.

1. Tai Chi Chuan Ching (attributed to Chang San-Feng)

- As you move, your movements should be continuous and flowing, without stopping and starting.
- When one part moves, all parts move.

- When one part is still, all parts are still.

Try not to take all these too literally; like all the advice in the Classics, these are guidelines that are not necessarily to be followed to the letter. They help to aim us in our training in a certain direction — not so that we reach the target, but so that we walk the right path. Similarly, when we talk about the myths and legends of Tai Chi, these are like biblical stories and should not be taken literally. They are metaphors, parables, and allegories that are there to inspire us and keep us motivated in our practice.

2. The Treatise on T'ai Chi Ch'uan (attributed to Wang Tsung-yueh)

- Avoid leaning in any direction.
- Keep your body upright.

3. Expositions of Insights into the Practice of the Thirteen Postures by Wu Yu-hsiang

- Be still as a mountain.
- Move like a great river.
- Walk like a cat.

4. Yang's Ten Important Points by Yang Cheng-fu

- Keep the head up (i.e. don't study your feet)
- Don't inflate the chest
- Keep the waist loose (ie. knees flexed)
- Keep shoulders and elbows low
- Go slow

I see what you mean by being vague. Are there any other texts that might help?

There is one book that is not generally included with the Classics, but it is referred to by many Tai Chi teachers across the world for its insights and applications to our contemporary world, and that is the ancient philosophical text known as the ***Tao Te Ching***.

What's that, and can I get a copy online?

Written by a man named Lao Tzu (though it is now thought there was more than one author), it is a book of poetic short chapters that underpin the basic patterns of movement in nature. These reflections or observations explore the relationship we have with our environment, our community, our country, and our planet. If you pick up a copy, you will no doubt recognise quite a few of these snippets of wisdom, such as bending like bamboo in the wind, or not trying to stand too tall in case you should topple over.

These simple, observable rules of nature are ingrained in many of the movements of Tai Chi, and for this reason, many instructors refer students to this book. The Tao Te Ching encourages readers to observe, adapt, and harmonize with life's inevitable ebbs and flows. Its timeless insights provide a fresh perspective on resilience, balance, and simplicity in everyday practice. And yes, copies are available in digital, paperback, and even audio versions everywhere. See References at the end of the book for a couple I particularly recommend.

Any final tips?

Well, I don't want to hold you back any further from starting your practice, but there are a couple of tips I'd personally recommend.

1. Take your time. Don't rush. It's a **quality,** not quantity, thing, so try not to do everything at the beginning. Get an overall picture of what we are doing before trying each of the moves. Some teachers chant, 'Practice, Practice Practice' to their students. I prefer, 'Patience, Patience, Patience'.

2. Keep the knees and elbows **soft** (unlocked) so that your centre can move with greater freedom and flow. A flexible waist is the starting point of all our moves. Let your arms follow the waist.

6

FINAL WORDS

That was all really vague!

I know, but it's important to understand that these moves have their origins in the ideas and practices of the past. Knowing something of this history and culture empowers you to work creatively in developing your own practice today. Try not to think about it too much. As you work through the different postures, we'll be looking at how some of these principles can help us learn the moves. So for now, put them to one side, and let's move on.

Can we get on with the moves now?

Yes, let's start by breaking down the moves into their foot and arm patterns.

SECTION III: THE FUNDAMENTAL MOVES

"I move, therefore I am."

HARUKI MURAKAMI

INTRODUCTION TO SECTION III

What are we going to be doing in this section?

I am going to begin your training by teaching you the basic foot and arm positions for each of the postures, so that when you move on to the following two sections, you'll already be familiar with much of what you need to learn. This will help you relax more in the final postures, which can be demanding on your coordination, balance, breathing, and timing.

We will begin with the standard footwork patterns that you will find repeated again and again in all Tai Chi styles. After that, we will look at basic arm movements and one in particular: Passing Palms.

Passing Palms: When two opposites pass by. Seen
from two angles.

Any Final Tips?

- Try to practise just the eight footwork patterns until they
  feel comfortable to you before moving on to the arms.
- Take your time.
- Enjoy the simplicity of the moves.
- Don't try to memorise the moves. Let your body and
  mind relax as you practise. We'll be coming back to them
  all later.

OK, if you understood the Final Tips and are ready, then let's
begin.

7

THE BASIC 8 STEPPING PATTENS

In this section, you will be following one of the fundamental rules of movement in Tai Chi: You cannot pick up a foot before first emptying the weight from it. It may sound obvious, but we often walk, step, or even stumble around with weight still in the foot that we are picking up. This is a habit that we want to change. The following 8 foot patterns all begin by emptying, or removing, the weight from the leg before lifting it. If we want to glide from posture to posture in the effortless way we see Tai Chi players move, then we need to begin our training with this.

1. The step forward

Used in the postures: Brush Knee, Step and Punch, Four Corners and more.

*Step out with heel first with **no** weight in the foot. Then, slowly transfer weight from the back leg to the front.*

This is, undoubtedly, the most common step in Tai Chi. It is very simple to do. However, when I say simple, everything appears simple when you have been doing it for over 30 years. If this is your first time, you may want to take note of a few pointers:

- As you step forward, step slightly out to the side. Avoid stepping in a straight line.
- Your body weight is transferred slowly between one leg and the other. It is a gradual movement done with control.

- Try to avoid falling into the step; instead tentatively place a heel down first on the ground before slowly rolling the weight forward fully into the foot.
- Keep your knees unlocked throughout the move.
- Try to avoid bobbing up and down as much as possible. Imagine that as you step, your head is in contact with a low ceiling. Try to always keep this sense of contact in order to avoid rising and sinking too much.
- Once you have transferred the weight into the front leg, ensure the knee is over the centre of the foot. If you look down and you can't see the tips of your toes or the end of your shoe, you may be bending your knee too much!

2. The wide-step forward

Used in the posture: Diagonal Flying.

Same as Step forward but think wide rather than long.

In this variation of the above step, we not only step out in front and slightly to one side (as we did in the **Front Step**), but we also take an even wider step so that your heel goes out a little further to the side, touches the ground, and then gently eases the body weight from the back foot into the front leg. The key to performing this movement is to remember that it is not a longer step but a wider one to the side.

3. The heel step

Used in the postures: Play Guitar and Lifting Hands.

A very simple step begins by focusing your attention entirely on one leg, which will gently move forward. Slowly and with precision, lift this leg from the hip, ensuring the motion is smooth and controlled rather than rushed or jerky. Extend the leg forward just enough so the heel can reach the ground without strain. As you begin to lower the leg, pay attention to the sequence of movement: the heel touches the ground first—gently, lightly—almost as if you were testing the surface. Make sure that only the heel makes contact at this stage, while the toes remain lifted and relaxed.

At the same time, consciously keep almost all your body weight on the back leg, which acts as your anchor. The back leg should remain strong but relaxed, with the knee slightly bent, never locked, to maintain a sense of balance and readiness. The front knee, too, should remain soft, allowing for flexibility and flow in your posture. Avoid locking the joints, as this restricts the movement and disrupts the natural energy flow.

Same technique as step forward but without transferring weight. Can you place the heel down and keep weight in back leg?

This movement should feel steady and deliberate, not forced. Imagine the sensation of planting a seed, with the heel grounding gently into the earth while the rest of your body remains balanced and poised. Take a moment to ensure your upper body stays upright, your shoulders relaxed, and your breath calm, allowing the movement to flow seamlessly into the next step. Practice this slowly until the coordination of weight distribution and gentle heel placement becomes second nature.

4. The toe step

Used in the posture: White Crane Spreads Its Wings.

This is almost the same as the **Heel Step**, but instead of the heel touching the floor, it is the ball of the foot. Once again, most of the weight remains on the back leg. Use the same instructions for Heel Step but replace Heel with the ball of the foot.

Toe Step: From front, then side and showing use in White Crane Posture

5. The step back

Used in the postures: Repulse Monkey and Golden Rooster and some of the transition moves in the Extra Moves in Section VI

The step back in Tai Chi is most frequently observed in the *Step Back to Repulse the Monkey* sequence, that appears in most Tai Chi forms. At times it appears as a single move, other times it is repeated three or five times, depending on the style.

Stepping back: Images begin on left (start here) and end at right.

- Like the **Step Forward**, pick up one foot slowly, but this time, move it behind.
- Allow the toes to touch the ground first.
- Roll the weight slowly into the foot, and then into the entire leg.
- Try to step back, leaving approximately shoulder-width distance.

6. The side step

Used in the posture: Waving Hands.

The side step is only found in the sequence known as *Waving Hands in Clouds*, though it appears additionally in many of the traditional Tai Chi warm-up exercises that loosen the waist and teach us body weight coordination. For that reason alone, it is an important move.

Images start at left and finish at right: Feet together, separate, shift weight, feet back together. Then try and go back the other way.

This simple shuffle is triggered by a turn of the waist. By turning the waist to one side and then back the other way, the feet follow and shuffle along. The secret to this move is the turn of the waist, for when we turn, we move the weight into that side of the body, freeing up the other leg to step out or step in. Try it by just following the weight and the turn of the hips.

7. The cross step

Used in the postures: First Corner, Step and Punch and transition moves in our Extended Form.

A simple step that often leads into a simple step forward as a follow up move.

Cross-step from side: Point the toes out, place the foot down, and raise the back heel.

As the name implies, this move involves a step across the body, with the toes turned outward as though you are preparing to land on the outer edge of the foot. The key is to create a sense of balance and direction as you step. For example, if you are cross-stepping with your right leg, your toes should naturally turn out to the right, creating a stable base for the next movement. Similarly, when using your left leg, the toes will point outward to the left. This outward positioning not only ensures proper alignment but also helps maintain fluidity and stability as you shift your weight. The turning of the toes outward is essential, as it opens the hips slightly, allowing for greater mobility and preparing the body for the subsequent transitions in the form. Remember to keep the step controlled and deliberate, as the intention behind each movement is as important as the physical action itself.

Cross step seen from the front using right. But remember it is important to practice these steps on both sides.

- Remember that whenever we use this step, we are in a transition between moves, so it is not held for very long before we step forward and conclude the move.
- Once again, gently place the foot on the ground at the appropriate angle.
- Slowly transfer the weight to that foot while preparing the other foot to **Step Forward** (by raising the back heel slightly).

8. The turning step

Used in the posture: Single Whip.

This move, although a little more complex, is one of the smoothest and most efficient transitional moves in Tai Chi. Spend a little time getting familiar with it, as it will enable you to turn 180 degrees with ease and fluidity. This foot pattern will help not only with your Tai Chi moves but also if you need to change direction quickly or in a small space.

1: Follow Images that start from left to right. Fingers point to foot positions and weight directions.

- Turning Step starts from a **Step Forward** position. Try it with the right foot forward.
- By putting all the weight on the back leg, we free up the front foot. Try to raise the front toes but leave the heel in contact with the ground.
- Now, by turning the waist to the left, the front foot turns too. (Swivelling on the heel as far as it can.) Now place the whole foot on the ground.
- Shift the weight back into this (temporarily twisted) front right foot.
- Continue turning the waist to the left again, swivelling this time on the ball of the left foot, heel slightly raised off the floor.

- Complete your turning of the waist by picking up the raised left foot and stepping out slightly to the side.
- Transfer the weight into this foot and check that your knee is positioned correctly above the centre of the foot.

2: Turning Step-images continue from left to right. Note final turn of right foot at very end.

How was that? Confusing? Just go back over each stage, step by step. Look at the images and check out the video links at the back of the book for demonstrations of all these moves.

Still not sure and would like to see the moves in action? No problem as there are plenty more resources available. You can either jump over to the online course and watch this section in the course as I demonstrate these each of these foot movements. Or if you prefer not to do that, then check out the links at the back of the book for other online examples of these moves.

Finally, as I mentioned at the beginning, take a little time to get used to these steps. It is worth spending a little time getting used to them. Learning them now will make the postures much easier, and, more importantly, they will begin retraining your body to move more efficiently and smoothly in your daily life.

So go back over the sequence now and practice all eight patterns again before moving on to the next chapter.

8

THE BASIC 5 HAND PATTERNS

Now that you have learned the footwork, I want to introduce some of the upper-body arm patterns that frequently in the Tai Chi postures. None of them are very complicated, and some of the instructions may appear obvious to those of you who have practised a little before or done a similar martial art. However, do take a look at them, as they embrace some of the most important rules in Tai Chi.

The first important rule is to keep your shoulders and elbows down (not raised) whenever possible. Raising the elbows or shoulders immediately creates tension in the shoulder, neck, and upper body that will inhibit your movements and prevent the feeling of flow and looseness between the postures. To understand this concept, try this exercise:

How to raise your arm without tension

- Put your left hand on your right shoulder.
- Now bend your right arm and raise your right wrist to the level of your shoulder, and then raise the elbow out to the side until it's also level with your shoulder.
- Can you feel the shoulder and back of the neck tense up?

Simple elbow re-position can cut down upper body tension

Now let's try it again:

- Put your left hand on your right shoulder. (Same as before.)
- Now bend your right arm and raise your right wrist as before. Then raise your elbow to the side, just like before.

- Now, keep your wrist at the same height, but drop your right elbow so that it points down.
- Can you feel your shoulder relax again?

These are some of the simple rules that we want our bodies to learn. So try out each of the five hand positions now.

1. Forming a fist

Used in the posture: Step and Punch.

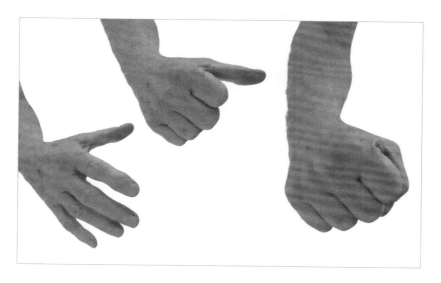

Unlike some other martial arts, the fist in Tai Chi is held loose, not tight, with the thumb on the outside of the fingers (never inside the curled fingers). Try to avoid clenching the fist as though it were something that needed to be kept hard. Imagine that there is still a small amount of space between the palm and the curled-up fingers.

2. The push hand

Used in the postures: Repulse Monkey, Play Guitar, Lift Hands, Brush Knee, The Corners and more.

A very simple position of an open, relaxed hand with fingers that are slightly separated and naturally curved. If you are thinking of a 'karate chop' image, then put that to one side, as it contrasts entirely with the softness required in Tai Chi. In Tai Chi, it is important that the wrist is relaxed and not tightly angled, as this creates unnecessary tension in the forearm, upper arm, and shoulder. Such tension can also encourage us to lock the elbow, restricting fluid movement. These are all things we try to avoid as we perform our moves in the Form, where relaxation, flow, and proper alignment are fundamental principles.

3. The hook hand

Used in the posture: Single Whip.

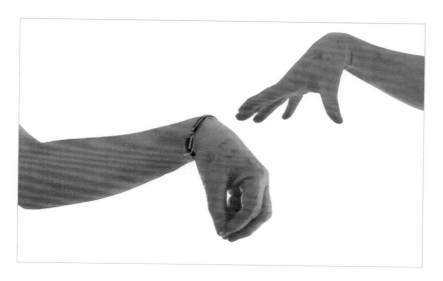

An iconic hand position in Tai Chi and one you will see at the end of an outstretched arm on many a poster advertising a Tai Chi class. The hand position is also known as the **Dragon's fist**. This unusual hand position is formed by bending the wrist and dropping the fingers and thumb underneath the wrist so that they all connect with each other.

This move is only seen in the posture called *Single Whip,* or its variations such as *Squatting Single Whip,* sometimes referred to a *Snake Creeps Through Grass.* It accompanies the **Turning Step** that we looked at in the last chapter.

4. Pressing down (holding on to the chair)

Used in the postures: White Crane, Golden Rooster, Step and Punch and Diagonal Flying.

Note how the hands appear to be finding support on either side.

This hand position is often overlooked in the Form, as our attention is focused on the other side, which is playing a more active role in a defence or attacking move. However, the Pressing Down side (imagine holding on to the top of a chair or table top) provides a balance to the activity of the other arm. Paying attention to the Pressing Down movement provides a greater sense of stability, for example, when standing momentarily on one leg. Again, don't bend the wrist too far, as this will cause tension.

5. Waving hands

Used in the posture: Waving Hands in Clouds.

This iconic posture seen in all styles of Tai Chi primarily consists of following the turning movements of the waist and accompanies the Side Step footwork we looked at in the last chapter. When the waist is turned, the weight will shift from one leg to the other, and the arms will follow the body as though drifting through clouds.

Note how as the waist slowly turns, one hand moves up, while the other moves down

- Both hands follow their own circles.
- The palm facing down, when above.
- The palm facing up, when below.

Some people learn better using visual imagery, so try this: Imagine a car windscreen in front of you. Now, imagine both the wipers are angled towards the very centre and will be moving out. Picture the right one moving out first, but it doesn't come back; instead, it completes a full circle before returning to the middle. Once it has completed a circle, the left takes over and does the same, moving out to the left, down, and back, having completed a circle.

This is all we are doing with Waving Hands. The circles begin hesitantly, but after a while they begin to blend as we move from one side to the other. Start with single circles and then let them move more naturally and with a greater sense of relaxation.

As you did with the foot patterns, practice each of the hand positions in this chapter until you are familiar with them all. You don't need to memorise them; just get to know them so that, when called upon, you will recognise the shape and be able to roughly copy it. For examples of these moves online, check the Reference section at the back of the book.

When you are ready, we will move on to the final chapter in this section: **Passing Palms**.

9

THE NOTION OF PASSING PALMS

Many of the moves in Tai Chi are about finding balance. In the pursuit of balance, the moves explore shifting from one "opposite" to another. Such as where a move shifts between...

- Left and Right
- Up and Down
- In and Out
- Forward and Back

All the Tai Chi moves play with these "opposites," and each posture is made up of an interchange between the two. In fact, there is an entire theory about how they relate to one another, and this is called the Yin-Yang theory. Its popular iconic representation is made up of a circle with both a black and white shape inside that is always turning, always shifting between one or the other.

Yin Yang symbolizes the interplay of soft and hard, warm and cold, light and heavy, dark and light, male and female. In fact, according to Taoist philosophy, Yin Yang theory encompasses all the relationships in the universe (something it refers to as the 10,000 things), illustrating the infinite connections between contrasting forces.

This idea of an interplay of opposites, this shifting energy between one pole and another, appears within each posture, between transitions, and even in the pauses we take. It teaches us that opposites are not in conflict but exist to complement and balance each other. But there is one particular moment when this relationship becomes very focused, and that moment I call the **Passing Palms**, a striking expression of this dynamic interplay.

DIAGONAL FLYING

Diagonal Flying is one of the moves in which you can practice the Passing of Palms

How will I recognise the Passing Palms?

In many Qigong (breathing exercises), you will often see the hands passing close to one another, and, as they pass by, you may feel a tingling or magnetic force between them. This happens to a lot of practitioners as they relax into the moves and think less about the mechanical techniques and more of the sensations. Don't worry if it doesn't happen right at the beginning; give it time and just relax more, paying attention to what is happening on a sensory as well as a mechanical level.

In Tai Chi, as in QiGong, there are several postures in which the hands pass close by one another, particularly when the palms are open. Each open hand may represent an opposite: empty or full, hard or soft, rising or sinking, and, obviously, left or right.

So as you are about to learn the moves, pay special attention when one of these moments arrives. I'll remind you when the palms are about to pass. As they do, try to focus on the centre of each palm and see if you notice any feelings or sensations that arise between them. Obviously, at the beginning you will be concentrating on the mechanics of the move, but after a time, as you relax into the moves, try to focus on the palms, then on the fingers, and finally on the fingertips. You may experience an attraction or even a repelling of energy as the palms pass each other.

10

FINAL WORDS

Are we going to learn the full postures now?

Yes, you have now completed all your initial training and have graduated in the following subjects:

1. The history and nature of the Tai Chi Form

2. What the wise ones tell us about how best to learn the moves

3. The basic step and hand patterns for the moves

Congratulations. You are now ready to begin to learn the moves that make up the Form.

Can I go back and practise the footwork again first?

Of course, you can. It's much better to get the groundwork right at this stage before moving on. If, for any reason, you are thinking, "Ooh, I don't know, maybe I should take my time and go back and repeat the first few sections," then do that.

Take your time. By now, hopefully you will have learned something about the correct pace for your training. As you discover more and more about this, adapt and structure your learning of the Form to match your own pace, repeating as little or as much as you need. Only when you are ready, move on to the next section.

SECTION IV: POSTURES 1 - 5

"We are never more fully alive, more completely ourselves, or more deeply engrossed in anything than when we are playing."

CHARLES SCHAEFER

INTRODUCTION TO MOVES 1 - 5

The first section of our Tai Chi Form includes five beautiful moves. For each, you will learn the mechanics of the move before delving deeper into its meaning and placement within the Form.

When learning the postures, should I learn more than one at a time?

It's tempting to try to learn more than one at a time, but try not to. What seems easy at first will slowly become more challenging, and then you might be tempted to do something silly like give up. And we don't want that. Start slowly, and remember to have patience when learning Tai Chi.

How long will it take me to learn each posture?

How much motivation, energy, enthusiasm, and free time do you have? Only you can answer that. But as I keep saying, have patience. Try to allow at least a full day for each new posture.

Learning the mechanics—where your foot goes and where your arms are—is the simple part. Time allows you to feel how the move flows and accustoms your body to holding itself in a new way. If one day isn't enough, take two, three, or even a week. Most students in a local class follow a traditional pattern of learning a single posture each week. But you don't have to follow the pace of your teachers or other students; it's all up to you. If you're ever unsure, go slow. A slower, more mindful pace allows the real benefits to emerge.

STEP FORM

Will I be learning all 10 moves in this section?

You will be starting the ten, but in this section we will focus first five moves of our Form. Take your time with them and savour the unique flavour each posture offers.

Will I be learning the martial application of each move too?

Although the martial applications may interest you, their correct interpretation is often contested and debated within the Tai Chi world. There's little consensus on what each move is for or how it's best applied, though many teachers claim they hold the correct interpretation. Try not to take these people too seriously; we all fall into easy theories and interpretations at times. As someone who came to Tai Chi after practising other martial arts, I've fallen into the same trap.

The truth is that each school sees something different in each move, and each teacher has their own application. While there may be a coherent explanation for a move, that doesn't guarantee its effectiveness in a real fighting situation. Keep in mind that the fighting elements of Tai Chi don't resemble the same moves we practise in the Form—they must be adapted to a constantly changing and fluid situation. They are two closely related practices with different outcomes, so it's best not to focus on applications here. Instead, let's focus on developing rhythm and flow, the feel of the moves, and their symbolism, rather than random interpretations of their possible use in combat.

Fair enough, but can we get on with the moves now?

OK, let's begin.

11

WHITE CRANE SPREADS ITS WINGS

Our first posture in this Short Form is called *White Crane Spreads its Wings*. It's a simple move to learn, as you will soon discover. Let's go straight into the move, and afterward, I can explain what it means and why we have started with this posture.

Recognise the toe-step we did earlier?

How to do: White Crane Spreads its Wings

- Start from a standing position, with the feet shoulder-width apart and the knees slightly flexed. Allow your arms to hang loose at your sides while your head faces forward.
- Shift your weight into your right leg.
- Step forward with the left foot into a **Toe Step**.
- Raise the right hand so the palm turns outward, as though shielding your eyes from the sun.
- Keep the wrist up but the elbow low.
- Your left hand pushes down to the side.

From this side you can see the left hand pressing down

Any final tips?

1. In the Tai Chi Classics, Chang San Feng wrote:

> "When one part moves, all parts move, and when one part is
> still, all parts are still."

White Crane Spreads Wings is a good illustration of what he was
referring to. As the right arm rises, the left drops, and at the same
time, the leg moves out. Ideally, all these things are happening at

the same time, each limb travelling at a slightly different pace. This may prove tricky at the beginning, so have patience. As you get familiar with the move and the way we move in Tai Chi, this coordination skill will manifest itself over time.

2. Remember that the Toe Step does not carry weight, so check to see if you can lift that front foot **without** having to transfer weight out of the leg first. Can you do it?

3. Check out the **Resource Section** at the back of this book for video examples of all these moves as well as 360 degree motion images of each of the postures.

Open up your wings and feel the energy spread around you

Why is it important and what does it signify?

The White Crane symbolises a bridge between the land of mortals and the home of the Taoist Immortals. According to legend, the White Crane was the only animal that could pass between the two worlds. You may remember that it was a White Crane that transported Chang San Feng up to the Pink Palace to receive his Immortality award. Now you may be asking yourself, "**Immortality**, what on earth has this to do with Tai Chi?" Let me clarify what the Taoist concept of Immortality means for us today:

- The capacity for the body and mind to completely engage with each unfolding moment of every day.
- To be able to live fully in the present and not get distracted or worried about what has happened or what might happen.
- It is about connecting with the greater patterns and cycles of nature and seeing yourself as an integral part of those processes.
- It is about letting go of our sense of ourselves as something separate, as an individual ego stamping around, complaining that the world isn't what it ought to be.
- Immortality is recognising that some things are beyond our control, and that actually might not be a bad thing.

The Taoist Immortals were merely those who had managed to do this in their own charismatic way. If you'd like to know more about the Taoist Immortals or the Taoist concept of **Immortality**, I will include links to extra videos and books in the reference section at the end of this book.

Are all the postures going to be as easy as the White Crane?

Not necessarily, although if you have learned the footwork and arm patterns, this will make the following moves a lot easier.

Before we move on, I want you to spend a little time getting familiar with the White Crane posture. Play with it, see how it feels to do and experiment with it. Give it time to live within you. Open your wings and yourself to that greater energy and force, and by doing so, bring your attention and presence back into the present.

When you are ready, we will move on to the next posture.

12

STEP BACK TO REPULSE THE MONKEY

Our second posture is the evocatively named *Step Back to Repulse the Monkey*. First, have a go at learning the mechanics of the move, then we will look at what it means and why the Monkey posture appears here.

How to do: Step Back to Repulse the Monkey

Start from the end of *White Crane Spreads its Wings*.

Start right (previous move top right corner). Using the turning of the body, drop arms, raise arms, step back, push.

- Turn the waist to the right.
- Allow the right arm to swing down and the left to swing up until both arms are momentarily suspended at shoulder level—the right hand's fingers pointing back and the left pointing forward.
- Step back with the left foot (as now there is no weight in the leg). Touch the floor with the toes, but don't transfer the weight just yet.
- Now, turn the waist back to the front, and as you do so, bend the right arm so that the right hand moves close to the right ear.

STEP BACK TO REPULSE THE MONKEY   79

- Now, transfer the weight to the left foot.
- The right arm pushes to the front centre line. (Look out for **Passing Palms**.)
- The left arm settles at the left hip, palm up.
- Want to see the move in action? Check out the resources section for video links.

Close up view of Repulse Monkey from other side (left to right)
Small images show intermediate steps.

Any other tips?

- Once more, everything starts with the waist. This move consists primarily of a waist turn to the right, and then the waist turns back again, with the arms following the twisting motions of the waist in an opening and closing sequence.
- Try to allow the arms to move freely, swinging low and

rising again with the turn. Imagine them as heavy objects that swing in a pendulum-like way.

- Did you notice that there is a balance here, another Yin/Yang tension between the right and left sides? Imagine, as you begin, that you are pulling down the right arm and pushing up with the left. Then, as you complete the move, you are pulling something back with your left hand while pushing out with your right hand.
- And don't forget that **Passing Palms** moment.

REPULSE
THE
MONKEY

Why is it important and what does it signify?

In the Tao Te Ching, we read that:

> "The masters hang back
>
> That's why they're ahead of the game."

(RON HOGAN EDITION; SEE
REFERENCES)

The monkey can signify many things to different cultures:

- The mindless chatter that goes on daily in our heads.
- The dependence on opium consumption that consumed China until the early part of the last century.
- The monkey also reminds us that as soon as we begin anything, we should always be ready to step back if needed. Not to rush ahead, not to stay on stage or in the limelight, but to use every moment to reconsider, to think again, or simply allow others to step forward, giving us time to ponder whether we are taking things too seriously.

"If you ever start taking things too seriously, just remember that we are talking monkeys on an organic spaceship flying through the universe."

J. ROGAN

In Taoism, this act of stepping back is called **Learn to lead from behind,** and there are many Chinese folk stories of the importance of doing so, including the tale of the Immortal Taoist called Chang Kuo Lao, who was renowned for his long beard, his hat made from a cabbage leaf, and his trusty mule that Chang Kuo Lao could fold into a hanky and store in his back pocket.

Find out more about the Taoist Immortals in the **Complete Tai Chi** course that covers Chinese art, culture, and, the evolution of

Taoism. You can see one of the stories about Chuang Tzu and the Cock Fighter on my Youtube channel.

Enjoy the practice of both the White Crane and the Monkey together, and when you have practised the two, move on to the next posture: Play Guitar.

13

PLAY THE GUITAR

Our third posture in the sequence is called *Play Guitar*, or you may find it written as the *Play the Lute* or *Play the Pipa*. Let's first look at the simple parts of the move, and then we'll explore what it means and why *Play Guitar* appears here.

PLAY GUITAR

How to do: Play Guitar

(Start from the end of Repulse Monkey)

Side View. Images start at left moving to the right. Small images show intermediate steps.

- Drop both arms to your sides and move all your weight into your right foot.
- As the weight shifts, raise the heel of your left foot.
- Bring the right hand up under your right armpit, then push it forward to the centre of your chest.

- Swing your left arm forward so that it extends out in front of you, finishing ahead of the right. (See the centre image above.)
- The left foot steps forward into a **Heel Step** with the toes up.
- Both palms end up facing towards the centre, with the right palm looking towards the left elbow joint.
- All the weight is now on the right foot.

Front view. This time, images start at left and move right. Play Guitar

Any other tips?

The arms should feel as if the left is rising while the right rises momentarily before pushing forward and slightly down to the centre.

Remember the Classics again? All limbs move at the same time and then come to rest at the same time.

Why is it important and what does it signify?

Play Guitar reminds us that it is in playing, not studying, that we learn best. It's okay to not get everything right when we start out learning something new. Even failure is something to embrace rather than fight against, as long as we are on the slow path of learning. What's important in Tai Chi is not to try too hard, because when we try too hard, we don't relax and so miss out on all the important things that arise spontaneously as we train.

Musicians learn to play instruments, and we too learn to play with the rhythms and patterns of our body and mind. We have to remember not to turn the learning process into a chore or a ritual, thereby losing the spontaneity and joy of acquiring new skills.

Play Guitar shown on both sides.

Try to spend a little time getting familiar with the *Play Guitar* posture, and then when you are confident you have it, add it to the previous two and work on all three together. When you are ready, we will move on to the next posture: **Brush Knee and Push**.

14

BRUSH KNEE AND PUSH

Our fourth posture in this section is called *Brush Knee and Push*, and it resembles, literally, brushing the knee with one hand while pushing forward with the other. Let's go straight into the mechanical instructions.

BRUSH KNEE

How to do Brush Knee and Push

(Start from the end of Play Guitar)

Small image shows previous posture. Arms follow waist. And as you turn back to face the front, step out a little with the left foot.

Brush Knee: Turn, Step out, and Push.

- Turn your waist to the right and sweep the left arm across your body with the elbow low and the hand high. Can you feel the connection between the waist turning and the left arms moving across?
- Drop the right arm and allow it to swing down and up toward your right ear (similar to what you did with *Repulse Monkey*).

- Turn your waist back to the left and step forward and out to the side with your left leg.
- As you move your weight gradually into the left foot, allow the left arm to drop down across the body and let the hand to (metaphorically) brush the knee. As the waist turns back to the front, can you feel the connection between the waist turn and the movement of the left arms?
- The right arm moves on from the ear and pushes forward toward the centre line of your chest. The energy for this push arises from the transfer of weight from the back leg to the front.

Any final tips?

- *Brush Knee and Push* is a basic drill in Tai Chi and, once learned, can be repeated again and again on both sides, either as a stationary exercise or with a step forward each time. It is also a great exercise to do with a partner, each maintaining contact all the time with the arms, forming circles that move around and around.
- Keep the shoulders and elbows low: As you raise one arm, try to keep your shoulder relaxed and your elbow low, even though your wrist and hand may be held high. This will help maintain the fluidity of the move

and prevent your shoulder and neck from becoming tense.

- When finalising the push, keep the wrist soft, not tense.
- Confused about the arms and body weight? Look at the photos and follow just one arm. See how it moves in a circle? Now follow the other.
- Another tip: Wherever the arms are, the weight of the body is there too. Arms at the front? Then the weight is on the front leg. Arms at the back? Then the weight is on the back leg. Arms in transition? Then the weight moves from one foot to the other. It is a rule that cannot be applied to all Tai Chi moves, but it works here with *Brush Knee*.

Why is it important and what does it signify?

Brush Knee is all about sweeping out the old, removing the unwanted baggage or dust from our lives, and learning to travel lighter and with less weight (an idea that we will come across later in the move called Diagonal Flying).

Clearing away the dust or the things we no longer need teaches us to do more with less. As the German philosopher **Kant** wrote:

"We are not rich by what we possess, but what we can do without."

Spend a little time getting familiar with the posture. If you get confused with the move, go back to just working on the legs and footwork, and then add the arms.

Still not sure? It's understandable. This is one of the moves that students find most difficult to grasp. But persevere, as it's one of the fundamental moves of all styles and teaches us about posture, movement, and relaxation. If needed, check out the **Resource** section and watch it demonstrated there.

Play with the move, see how it feels, experiment with it, and then add it to the others in your set.

1. White Crane
2. Step Back to Repulse the Monkey
3. Play Guitar
4. Brush Knee and Push

BRUSH
KNEE

When you are ready, move onto the final posture in this section: Step and Punch.

15

STEP AND PUNCH

Our fifth and final posture in this section is called *Step Forward, Deflect Downwards, Intercept, and Punch,* or more simply, *Step and Punch.* Let's take a look at the mechanics of the move.

STEP FORWARD DEFLECT DOWN AND PUNCH

How to do Step and Punch

(*Start from the end of Brush Knee*)

- Take your weight off the left foot and raise the toes.
- Sit back into the right leg.
- Drop the hands in front of you.
- Return your weight into the left foot once more, open your left palm, and with your right hand, form a Tai Chi fist.
- Bring your right foot alongside your left and keep the right heel off the ground. Just the ball of the foot is in contact with the floor, and the weight stays in the left foot.
- Pick up the right leg as though to step out to the right (**Cross-step** position).
- At the same time that you pick up your foot, turn out your right forearm and fist.
- Let the open palm follow alongside the right fist.
- As you move your weight into the right foot that is now on the ground, begin to separate the right and left arms. The right hand moves to the right hip as an upturned fist, while the left arm stretches forward as an open hand.
- Step forward with the left foot, and as you transfer the weight, bring the right arm forward into the centre-line

with the right hand now forming a vertical fist, while the left arm bends until the left open palm ends up close to the right elbow.

From left to right seen from front view: Step and Punch includes 3 steps: (1) Bring feet together, (2) Cross-step then (3) Step Forward

Any other tips?

- If you find this move challenging, that's because it involves two steps, large waist turns, some challenging balancing, and a martial-like punch at the end. It requires a little more coordination than some of the previous moves.
- If you still find the move a little difficult, try first to do the move without using your arms and just focus on the footwork. Remember, you bring the feet together first,

then move into the **Cross-step,** and finally finish with the **Forward-step**.

- When you have the feet worked out, add the arms. After first dropping the arms, remember that they move together with the leg as you raise the knee, then separate, then return with the punch.

From Left to Right: Close up of the Cross-step part of the move.

Why is it important and what does it signify?

Despite its clear martial conclusion, Step Forward to Deflect Down, Intercept, and Punch reminds us of the general principles of opening and closing. Can you feel this in the movement? Arms come together, then apart. Feet are together, then apart. One fist is closed (lightly) and the other is open.

Like the traditional Chinese salutation of a fist enclosed in a soft palm, there is a balance here between softness and hardness, between outer and inner, between open and closed.

Closed fist, open palm.

Intercepting is also known as "Parrying" in Tai Chi, and like many other Martial arts, the move consists of avoiding a direct block and instead choosing to deflect, redirect, or intercept the energy. This offers us a third way of looking at problems: Not to run away or confront them but instead to see if it is possible to work **with** the energy in order to redirect it to a more practical end (and less damaging).

Take your time with this move. It is a little more complicated, so practice it for a while before adding it to the others.

16

FINAL WORDS

Once you have added *Step and Punch* to your moves, you will have completed the first half of our Tai Chi Form.

Congratulations! 🙌

Try to practice this first section until it feels familiar. It is the first half of this course - the one side of the yin-yang symbol. The other side is coming up next.

If you can, put together all five moves, linking them one after another. Do this until they feel as though they flow into one another — like the turning symbiotic energy of the yin yang. Once you have done this, we can move on to the next section.

But remember, there is no rush. Repeat as much as you need to. Take your time. Play, don't study.

SECTION V: POSTURES 6-10

"I jump 'em from other writers, but I arrange 'em my own way"

BLIND WILLIE MCTELL

INTRODUCTION TO MOVES 6 - 10

Before we start this second section of the Form, I want you to select one of the following two ways to proceed:

1. If you are a fast learner and have learned the last 5 moves thoroughly, then add each of the following moves to your first 5 as we go along.
2. If you are having trouble remembering all the first 5, then my advice is to put these aside for the moment and just concentrate on the next 5. We can come back to the first 5 moves at the end and put them all together then.

It makes no difference to what we are doing in the book, as we are just going to be learning them one at a time. So, take a moment to think about which approach would best suit you.

Whatever option you choose, we will start this set with an easy move called *Diagonal Flying*.

17

DIAGONAL FLYING

Flying is often misunderstood as simply boarding a plane, hang-gliding during a weekend adventure holiday, or messing about with drones, but in Tai Chi, flying has another meaning—to travel without excessive baggage, to move around with a lightness of being. We were first introduced to this concept in *Brush Knee and Push*, but in *Diagonal Flying*, we will be exploring the concept a little more deeply. But before we get too involved in the meaning, let's look at the move so you can feel what it's like to do and then after, we'll come back to its meaning.

DIAGONAL FLYING

How to do: Diagonal Flying

(*Start from the end of the last posture:* Step and Punch)

- Bring your right foot alongside the left again, similar to the way you began the Step and Punch move.
- Turn the waist to the left and let the left hand float up a little, palm facing down.
- Drop the right hand under the left as if you were holding a beach ball between your hands.

Start Right: Feet together, step wide, turn waist, separate arms.

- Take a forward **Wide Step** out to the right. Don't worry about stepping forward as much as stepping **out** to the side. This will make the move a bit easier for you at the beginning.

Reminder to the wide step we practised before.

- The left hand presses down to the side (**Press**) while the right hand moves across the body in a large diagonal cutting motion.
- Passing Palms.
- Your eyes should follow the right palm as it moves diagonally across your body and finishes its trajectory slightly above shoulder height with the palm facing up.

Diagonal Flying incorporates "passing palms" - see photo above. 1. Step wide. 2. Separate arms. 3. Look into open palm (head height)

Any other tips?

- The above final photo was taken from ground height, so it looks like the right palm is higher than it is. It should end up level with your eyes.
- The right arm and the back of the hand form an almost straight line, but one with a slight curve. Imagine your arm as a warped piece of timber—straight but curved.
- Allow the right hand to curve naturally and the fingers to relax and separate slightly so that the air can move between the fingers and around the palm.
- Although it appears that the upper arm is doing everything, once again, it is the relationship between the two that creates the whole move.

- As in *Repulse Monkey*, each hand passes over the other and exchanges energy, as well as defining the purpose of each.
- If it helps, think of a large rubber band between the two hands. Even though they move in opposite directions, they are still intricately connected, and when one reaches the end of its path, it is compelled to return to its opposite position—Yin and Yang.

DIAGONAL FLYING

Why is it important and what does it signify?

Diagonal Flying (using the waist to step out to the side or onto the diagonal) speaks to us of being unfettered by physical things as well as attitudes and corrosive ideas that consume our energy but do little to nourish our soul. To fly, therefore, is to be able to go beyond these limits, to travel light with just hand baggage, thankful for the opportunity to discard the weightier nonsense that ties us down in life. It is also a move about taking bigger steps, boldly occupying space—whether buildings, a public square, or government buildings—while reminding us to stay light-footed and ready to move away if need be.

This lightness of touch is something we explore frequently in Tai Chi in a series of exercises referred to as Pushing Hands. One related exercise is called **Sticking,** where two people are connected by no-more than a single finger resting on the back of a hand. One person closes their eyes and follows the other, with just the lightest of contact, responding to the rhythms and movements of the other person. Have a look at this video on **Sticking.**

Now, practice this first move in this section, and when you are ready, move on to the next move: *Waving Hands in Clouds.*

18

WAVING HANDS IN THE CLOUDS

Waving Hands in Clouds, or *Waving Hands*, as it is more commonly referred to, is one of the most recognised and classic moves in Tai Chi. It's a beautiful move, both to watch and perform. So, let's get on with the mechanics of the move.

Start from Left. Step up so feet are parallel and turn waist slightly to right. Slowly turn waist to left, changing hand positions.

How to do: Waving Hands in Clouds

(*Start from the end of* Diagonal Flying)

- Turn your waist slightly to the right.
- As you do, shuffle your left foot forward so that it ends up parallel with your right foot
- Bring your left hand to your right hip, palm facing up.
- Turn and lower your right palm slightly so it rests above the left, as though you were holding a beach ball again (like at the beginning of *Diagonal Flying*).
- By turning the waist to the left, carry the beachball over to the left hip; as you turn, switch your hands over.
- Now that you have turned the waist to the left, your weight is on the left leg, and the left hand is now over the right.

- As you do all of this, bring the right foot in closer to the left.
- Then begin to reverse the move by turning the waist back to face the front
- Bring the beachball with you.
- Switch arms again so that the right is now on top and most of the weight has moved back into the right foot.

Remember the general rule: Arms follow the weight of the body. In Waving Hands the arms are following the turn of the waist.

Any other tips?

- You can also practice this posture as a drill by stepping out and carrying the ball across the room in one direction and then back again. See how many steps and waving hands you can do before you need to come back the other way.

- This description of the arms as carrying a beach ball gives you the idea of space, separation, and a slight curve of the arms. But once you have this idea, you can dispense with it and think instead of moving amongst the clouds drifting past on a lazy, hazy summer morning.
- The waist, as always, must turn first before the arms, legs, hands, body weight, or head move.
- The elbows should be kept low; otherwise, your shoulders and neck will tighten and inhibit your movement.
- Eyes: Follow the movement of each rising palm. When one begins to fall, switch your gaze to the other rising hand.

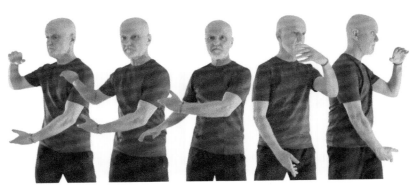

Waving Hands is more a waist move than an arm move.

Why is the move important and what does it signify?

Waving Hands teaches us the strength of yielding. In Tai Chi, we learn this as a practical exercise in giving way to a greater force. Yielding is often the result of following the movement of a circle or a spiral that is constantly changing shape like a drifting cloud. But these lazy, soft clouds can become thunder clouds too. Don't think

Tai Chi is just softness, for within the art there is the capacity to switch from soft to hard, light to heavy, or slow to fast, without tension and without losing your root.

Yielding is not always about physical force; it can also be practised in a discussion when you realise that winning every argument or debate isn't necessary. Neither is it necessary to dominate a discussion or force an idea on others. Yielding involves maintaining your centre by being grounded, and in so doing learn where the root and centre of the other person lies. And in that, there is great strength.

Play with the move and practice it as a drill, moving across your room and back again. Then, when you are confident with the posture, add it to Diagonal Flying.

19

GOLDEN ROOSTER STANDS ON ONE LEG

Golden Rooster Stands On One Leg is clearly a posture that talks to us about balance. But let's look at the mechanics first and then we will come back to the ideas that make up this move.

Golden Rooster seen from side. Note that the raised foot is relaxed and not held up in tension.

How to do: Golden Rooster

(*Start from the end of Waving Hands*)

- Move all your weight into the right foot.
- Drop the right hand, slowly pushing it down to the side.
- At the same time, bring the left hand up, fingers pointed to the sky (**Passing Palms**.)
- As the left hand moves up, imagine it is connected by string to your left knee.
- As the left hand rises, so too does the left knee, with the toes relaxed and dropped down.

FINAL TIPS

Any final tips?

- In this posture, it is important to feel the weight of the body in the feet. Allow your body weight to sink through you to the ground. You can achieve this by relaxing as much of your structure as possible. Identify areas of tension as you perform the moves, and focus on reducing that tightness.

- Imagine you are anchored to the floor like an oil rig out at sea or a windmill on land. Or imagine you are a tall oak tree, and your roots go down deep into the earth to hold you firm. Can you feel the qualities of solid and hollow, full and empty, here? Can you feel yourself sinking into your right leg as you raise your left knee?

- In some moves of Tai Chi, we move out while retreating or move in while expanding out. Here we are moving both down and up at the same time. Can you feel this as you sink into the leg yet rise with the other arm? Once more, there are beautiful opposites in play during our Form.

- For better balance, imagine your right hand holding onto a flat surface (**Press Down**) and avoid locking your right knee. Keep the knee slightly soft and open.

Watch for Passing Palms and Pressing Down

Why is it important and what does it signify?

"Keep your feet firmly planted,

unless you want to fall on your face."

CHAPTER 24 OF THE TAO TE CHING

The Chinese characters for the name of the posture suggest standing on the earth, standing up for oneself, becoming independent, and having confidence in one's vulnerability.

Now, this is curious: how can you have strength in vulnerability? Do you remember the example of yielding and clouds in the posture *Waving Hands*? Softness has the capacity to absorb and, if well grounded, can spring back when needed. What appears precarious is in fact suppleness, like bamboo blowing in the wind.

Although the posture is done from a position of balance and good grounding, the balance we are looking for in Tai Chi is to be found in movement, not stillness; it borrows from our natural curiosity to explore the boundaries of life through sinking and rising and through the interaction of full and empty. Here lies another definition of strength altogether.

As always, practice the move and add it to the previous two postures. When you are ready, join me in the next chapter for the classic move called *Single Whip*.

20

SINGLE WHIP

If I were to compose an album of Tai Chi's Greatest Hits, *Single Whip, Waving Hands,* and *Repulse Monkey* would, most likely make the top three. *Single Whip* is characterised by a 180° change of direction and, consequently, is a little more challenging than some of the earlier postures. For this reason, we will break down the footwork first before adding the arms.

How to do: Single Whip

(*Start from the end of Golden Rooster*)

Part 1: Feet and Waist Only

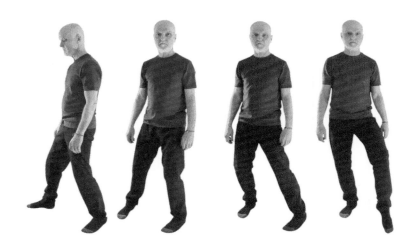

Start Left: Weight shifts from Right to Left and then back again.

- This move involves a waist turn of 180°. Although you will do this in stages and it may feel a little fragmented at the start, bear in mind that the final complete move is a flowing, smooth turn that brings you around to face the opposite direction.
- To start: Drop your left foot back onto the floor, but this time place it behind you (**Step Back**) and gradually place the weight into this leg.
- Raise the toes of the now empty front foot, but leave the heel in contact with the ground.
- Turn your waist to the left, bringing the right foot with you as far as possible while swivelling on the heel that

remains in contact with the floor. Then drop the toes
back onto the ground.

- Transfer the weight from the back foot to the front foot.
- Keep turning your waist slowly to the left. To enable this,
  raise the left heel off the ground, but keep your left toes in
  contact with the floor.
- Can you feel how this enables your body to turn further?
- Finally, when you can't move further without picking up
  your left foot, pick it up. Step out to the side and transfer
  the weight back into the left.
- Check your knee position—can you still see your toes?

Continuing - from left to right: Pick up foot, step out, transfer
weight.

Work through this routine again and again. It is crucial to get this
move right so that the turn is smooth and consistent. I would
suggest you practice the footwork only for this move throughout
the day. Practice in the kitchen, in the office, in the lounge, in the
vet's waiting room, or even in the supermarket—wherever you are

and whenever you get a moment to try it out. Keep practising until you feel comfortable with the footwork. Only then should you continue and add the arms.

Start from left: *Step back, turn hips, arms follow, turn in foot, now turn back, arms follow, hold ball, step around, push forward, hook out to side. (Small images are transitions)*

Part 2: Add The Arms

Let's go back to the end of *Golden Rooster* again. From there, step back and...

- Shift weight out of the front foot into the back.
- Rotate the waist to the left.
- Both arms follow the waist turn, with elbows bent slightly, and both palms facing down.
- As you did above, bring the right toes around as far as possible when you turn your waist and keep your heel in contact with the ground.

- When you cannot turn any further, shift the weight back onto the right foot. (Yes, I know it feels awkward, but bear with it.)
- As you shift the weight, the right arm bends and the hand moves to the centre of the chest. The wrist is slightly bent, and all the fingers have dropped below and are in contact with one another. This is called the **Hook Hand**. (Remember to check out the web links at the end of the book for videos and gifs of many of these moves).
- At the same time, the left hand curves under the Hook Hand at the level of the lower abdomen, palm open.
- Continue to rotate the waist to the left, by lifting the left heel off the floor. Keep the toes in contact with the ground. (Once more, do you see how the waist can move further when you do this?)
- Now, as you rotate the foot on the toes, continue turning the waist and extend your right arm out to the side with the Hook Hand. Can you feel the connection between the Hook moving out and the turn on the ball of the foot?
- Lift the left foot off the floor and step out further to the left.
- The left hand is raised to chest height, palm still facing in.
- Shift the weight into the left leg and straighten the right leg (not fully).
- Allow the toes of the right foot to rotate alongside the waist and knee.
- Turn the left palm out and press into an imaginary opponent's chest. (**Push**)

Keep Right hand as Hook hand. Left as Open Palm.

Any other tips?

- Note: In the above photo sequence, the final hook hand looks as though it is very high. But this is just from a low camera angle so that you can see angle of head as well as arms. The Hook Hand ends up slightly higher than shoulder height.
- As the right arm moves out with the Hook Hand, use the momentum to keep the hips moving, initially by swivelling on the ball of the left foot and then by lifting the foot and stepping out. This is all part of the same swinging energy that you will read about in Section 6.
- Like Waving Hands, this move is all about spirals, though at first you will be concerned mostly with the positioning of the feet and hands during the turn. Later, however, when you feel more comfortable with the move, you will

find another rhythm, one that is generated by the waist as the weight shifts with the spiralling energy in the body.

- Remember to do this move in two stages if you find it challenging. Practice the feet first, and only later add the arms.

Why does Single Whip appear to differ from style to style?

Single Whip does differ a little with each style of Tai Chi. If you do a search on YouTube you'll notice variations in the angle of the hips and width of the arms. However, the basic movements are fundamentally the same. Even amongst teachers of the same school, the ultimate expression of each posture depends on the individual and the reasons for practice. Once again, postures can have a martial, health, or even exhibition purpose. (There is an entire tradition within the martial arts of exhibition and public display that lends yet another perspective to these moves.)

SINGLE WHIP

What does the move signify?

Single Whip in the Tai Chi Form is about ups and downs, lefts and rights, opening and closing, gathering and releasing. It's about soft and hard, crests and troughs, and energy in the form of waves. Single Whip uses the wave-like energy of the whip, generated by the two arms but expressed as a single force. It's a dynamic move, employing a spiralling of the body that teaches us how to shift from one direction to another and how to move with less effort.

Why is this move important?

This is the move that enables you to shift direction with ease and harmony. To onlookers, it appears as though you are sliding rather than stepping, once you've mastered the footwork and weight transfer. Additionally, it's worth learning because this move is repeated many times in the longer Tai Chi forms, should you continue your practice.

Finally

When you feel confident with it—and don't be surprised if this move takes longer to learn than the others (this is normal; it's a complex move)—add it to the previous postures. Then, when you are ready, join me in the next chapter for the final posture in our series of 10.

21

1ST CORNER

THE CORNER

Although *First Corner* may not make it into the Greatest Hits Album, it's a move, like *Single Whip*, that teaches how to change direction and step out onto the diagonal. It can be repeated as a sequence or drill—like *Brush Knee, Step and Punch, Waving Hands*, and *Diagonal Flying*—and in a sequence of four, with each step moving out in a different direction, it's often used in demonstrations and exhibitions.

Why then are we only practising one direction?

Originally, Tai Chi was taught as a Long Form, consisting of hundreds of postures that took years to even grasp the basic mechanics. Repetitions of moves on both sides were common, but gradually, as the Short Forms became more popular and replaced the longer versions, the repetitions were reduced. This is why, in some styles today, you will see the Monkey repeated 5 times, in others 3 times, and in others just once.

The Corners are traditionally done four times—hence they are often referred to as the Four Corners—but like the Monkey or Brush Knee, we are going to practice just one here for simplicity: a single step to a single corner.

Is this move also called Fair Ladies or Fair Lady Weaves Shuttle?

Yes, however, as this is the only move in the Form that makes any explicit reference to gender and does so in such a traditionally role-cast way, some instructors have removed the reference and use either *Weaves Shuttle* by itself or *Travel to the Corners*. After all, we live in the twenty-first century, not the seventeenth, and we have a responsibility to ensure that it is not just our moves that evolve but our language as well.

From right to left: *Turn waist, bring round left arm to meet right. Then follow instruction below.*

How to do: First Corner

(*From the end of* Single Whip)

As this move consists of a change of direction (like Single Whip), we will break it down into two parts:

Basics, Part 1: Preparation

- Begin by turning your waist to the right and bringing your left arm around so the palm reaches your right elbow.
- This will feel awkward. As the weight shifts to your right leg, allow your left foot to turn on the heel with your waist and arms, just as you did in *Single Whip* using the **Turn Step**.
- Bend your right forearm so it moves into a vertical position, with the palm open and facing you.

- Then, shift the weight back into your left foot and slide the ball of your right foot a few inches back, closer to you, and toward your left foot.

Basics, Part 2: Completion

- Pick up your right foot (the one you've just slid closer to your body) and place it back on the ground, ensuring that the toes point outward to the right, as in the Cross-step movement.
- Gradually transfer your body weight onto this foot. Simultaneously, slide your left hand upward along the outside of your right forearm, keeping the motion smooth and controlled.
- Allow your left heel to lift gently off the ground, maintaining balance as you prepare for the next step.
- Step forward with your left leg into a Forward-step position, carefully transferring your weight onto this leg as you move.
- Raise your left hand to head height with the palm facing outward, keeping the fingers relaxed and slightly extended.
- Extend your right arm forward at chest height, pushing outward in a deliberate and steady motion. This concludes the Push movement.

After Cross step: Take final step forward to reach Corner.

Any other tips?

- There are two parts to this move: the preparation and the completion.
- The first part is the turn; adjust the arms and sit back into the left foot. You are in a state of preparation.
- The second part begins with the **Cross-step**, the follow-up step, and the extension of the arms. This is the completion.
- Imagine the first part as gathering your energy, your posture, and your intention. Imagine drawing into yourself all the resources you will need, then, like a spring, releasing all that energy with a turn of your waist, a step, and finally a push.

From right to left: *After completion, step back to centre and bring arms down.*

Why is it important and what does it signify?

"You can go far

if you don't have anything to carry."

(*TAO TE CHING: CHAPTER 22*)

Does this remind you of something? You may remember that we first came across a similar idea in the posture called *Diagonal Flying,* when we talked about the need to dispense with unnecessary baggage. Flying in this sense is about letting go of the unnecessary things that we tend to acquire, so that it becomes possible to travel light, unburdened by the heavy weight imposed on us living in the 21st century. It's a reminder to strip back the layers of complexity we impose on ourselves, allowing us to move with greater ease, freedom, and authenticity.

A wise person can travel long distances and still see every-thing she owns. She may be surrounded by beauty, but she isn't caught up in it."

TAO THE CHING: CHAPTER 26

As you will have deduced by now, I draw as much from the Tao Te Ching as I do from the Classics. There is a lot in Tai Chi that can be traced back to the ideas in the Tao Te Ching, and this is something that is shared by other martial arts too. Many other martial artists have used the book as a source of inspiration and guidance for their art. Bruce Lee often said that he felt it was the philosophy of Taoism that gave purpose and meaning to the moves and intentions behind much of his style, Jeet Kune Do.

Not surprisingly for a book that is several thousands years old, Tao the Ching has many versions on the market, including several specifically written for the Tai Chi student. If this interests you, take a look at the extra resources in this lecture.

Practice this move until you feel comfortable with it. Add it to the previous moves, and when you are ready, we will conclude this section of the Form.

22

FINAL WORDS

Congratulations! You have achieved something that many students have tried but failed to do. You have completed a Tai Chi sequence or Form. Many give up before completing the course, but you have made it this far. You have completed the fundamental moves and now have your 10 Step Form in place.

Remember to practice regularly until each move begins to feel like part of you. Otherwise, they will fade away, gradually disappearing into the distance. To prevent this, create a daily routine and choose a time of day to practice. Set a timer on your phone, if need be, to remind yourself to put aside a couple of minutes to run over the moves.

When you can do all the moves from 6—10 together, and you can see them flowing nicely into each other, add the original 5 until you have the complete set of 10.

That is your challenge now as we wrap up this section: to link all 10 moves together until you feel competent to go through them without too much difficulty.

Once you have done this, or if you have already been doing so throughout this section, then it is time to move on to the extra challenges in the final section of this book: **Walking Your Own Path**.

SECTION VI: WALKING YOUR OWN PATH

"Do not seek to follow in the footsteps of the men of old; seek what they sought."

—MATSUO BASHŌ

23

INTRODUCTION TO SECTION VI

WALKING YOUR OWN PATH

For some of you, learning all 10 postures will have been enough of a challenge, and now you may want nothing more than the opportunity to practice this small sequence of moves in your own time. If this is how you feel, then by all means read through the next section, but don't attempt any of the extra challenges yet, as each of them demands a whole new set of skills. Return to this section only when you feel confident and ready to move on.

The 7 Challenges

For those of you who are looking for an additional challenge, I have a series of new goals for you. Each of these challenges will resonate in different ways with different people. Read through the options and choose the path you wish to walk in this section.

There are 7 challenges here. Take your time reading over what each entails, and then make a choice as to how you wish your Form to develop. You do not need to take on all the challenges, though over time you may wish to come back and select a new one once you feel more confident with your Form. To begin, just pick one of the following 7 challenges and work through that.

1. Adding a beginning posture to your Form
2. Adding an ending posture to your Form
3. Repeating your Form, but on the other side (Mirroring)
4. Exploring transitions: How to move smoothly from one side to another
5. Expanding your Form by adding extra repetitions
6. Expanding your Form by adding new moves
7. Playing with rhythm and flow in your Form

What do you mean by "Make the Form yours"?

"Doing" Tai Chi is not like "doing" other tasks. As much as we may want it to be, it can't be reduced to a simple list of postures to tick off once performed. This is not what we mean by "doing" Tai Chi.

If we aspire to truly practice Tai Chi, then at some stage in our training, we must interpret the art to see how it relates to us individually, translating the practice in a way that is useful and applicable to the world around us: where we live, the air we breathe, and how our body functions in that environment. All of this affects how we practice the art. It's always interesting to know why people practiced Tai Chi in another era and another place, but we need tools that relate to where we live here and now. Given the average human attention span is shrinking by the hour, this is of utmost importance in the 21st century.

To make the Form progressive and forward-looking, paradoxically, we must go back to the beginning, back to how Yang Chen Fu applied and then adapted his grandfather's Form. He serves as our inspiration and precedent for converting our Form into what I call the "Elastic Form"—a form that adapts to the needs and practice conditions of where and who we are. Whether one day we have less time or energy, or more time and more energy, our Form will adapt accordingly.

Enjoy working through the 7 challenges. Why not start with the easier ones, such as adding a beginning or end to your Form? And remember, make full use of the resources section, which links to video and image examples of many of these. Good luck!

BEGINNINGS

Why do I need to learn a beginning and an end move?

You don't. But they serve to slow us down before starting and after finishing the Form. These Tai Chi moves vary from style to style, but what is important about the variations is not so much the superficial gestures as what lies behind them. This is true of all the postural differences between styles in Tai Chi.

The beginning move, whatever variation you practice, has a definite purpose: Is it to make the whole sequence look complete? Is it to make it look smooth and flowing? Or is it because if we spend a moment before we start to gather our thoughts, allow ourselves to relax, and let the games our mind plays dissipate as we concentrate on other things, we will benefit a hundredfold from the practice?

Feel the air move between the fingers as you begin

Challenge 1: Adding a beginning posture to your Form

All beginning moves give you time to:

- **Wait** for your weight to sink away from the top of your chest and down toward the ground.
- **Allow** your monkey mind to stop chatting.
- **Listen** for your breath to settle and deepen.
- **Feel** your muscles begin to relax.
- **Sense** your skin awaken to the air around you.

Then, when all is calm and your mind is alert, you will be ready.

TRADITIONAL
VERSUS
MODERN
LEARNING

The traditional step

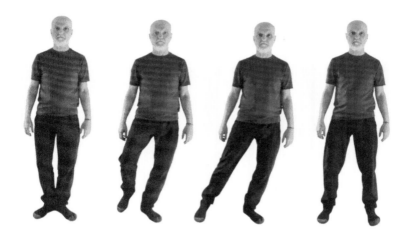

Start Left: Step out with left foot, feet parallel, shift weight.

Some schools begin with a traditional step. It starts with the heels together, followed by a series of small foot movements out to the side, turning the waist, opening the palms, turning the foot back in, turning the palms back in, and then raising your arms. This sequence is then reversed at the end of the Form.

The modern step

Modern: Start from shoulder width step, and raise and drop arms

Not surprisingly, other schools have chosen to bypass this ritual, simply stepping out to the side and then raising the arms in either a straight line or a circular move.

How does the teapotmonk start his Form?

I take my inspiration from the spiral movements that appear at the beginning of both the traditional Yang and Chen Forms. This small counter-clockwise spiral feels right for what is coming next. But this is a personal choice. You can see an example in the videos linked in the reference section. You may choose something else. Play, and in playing, discover another you.

NB: Want to see examples? Check out the online course for moving close-up examples.

25

ENDINGS

Challenge 2: Adding an ending posture to your Form

When concluding your Tai Chi Form, some schools reverse the traditional foot patterns at the start, accompanied by a move called *Cross Hands*.

Front View of X hands - a move that can you can see repeated several times in many tai chi forms.

Cross Hands is a common move to denote the completion of a Form, or part of a Form, and appears at several stages throughout both the Long Form and some variations of the Short Forms, depending on the school and specific style of Tai Chi.

Cross Hands is a simple posture to do: The arms complete two small circles, moving from the centre line and curling outward and downward. The arms then fold back into the centre, meeting at the wrists, level with the top of your chest. At this point, they can do several things, deepening on the posture that follows.

In some forms, this will be a move called *Embrace Tiger Return to Mountain*, that requires a big turning step and a push (see longer forms in resources section).

In our sequence, however, we are moving towards completion, so we turn the palms turn and allow them to float down to the sides, returning to where we began our Form.

Front view showing lowering of arms

Alternatively, you can use the spirals as I do, but finish by reversing the direction you started with. (This time, go clockwise.)

Finally, remember why you are doing any of this. It's not to fit more things into your day or to rush through the important stuff, but to do less, to slow down, to quiet your mind, and to find a little window of quality time that is yours in what may otherwise be a hectic timetable.

Part 1: Side view of Cross-hands to conclusion of Form

Don't just complete the final move and immediately return to what you were doing beforehand. Take a few moments to focus on how you feel now—your weight, your energy, your mind, and your breath. How do you feel? Let all of this come to your attention before moving on.

Part 2: Side view X Hands to conclusion.

NB: Want to see examples? Check out the online course for moving close-up examples.

26

MIRRORS

Challenge 3: Repeating your Form, but on the other side
(mirroring)

In many Tai Chi Forms some postures are repeated on both the
left and the right, but it is rare to find a Form that repeats all the
moves on both sides of the body.

What do you mean by both sides?

For example, I have shown you how to start with White Crane
Spreads it's Wings, and I have taught you to do the move by raising
your right arm, lowering your left, and pushing out your left foot.

This move could be done on the other side too, by raising your left arm, lowering your right, and pushing out your right foot. We call this mirroring in Tai Chi, and it can be repeated throughout the whole Form.

All postures can be repeated on both sides

Why are the postures not done on both sides?

In the rush to offer shorter Forms to the public, Tai Chi teachers reduced not only the repetitions of postures but skipped altogether performing the moves on both sides. For example, when Cheng Man Ching shortened the Yang Long Form to his very popular Short Form, he left out balancing a number of the moves. His version of Single Whip would only ever be performed with the left leg and hand forward and the whip arm thrust out on the right side. *Diagonal Flying, Step and Punch, Play Guitar,* etc. all fell victim to the one-sided bias of the specific Form.

Even today, many students of Tai Chi still only practice on one side, and when asked to repeat the move using the other arm or leg, they are unable to do so without a great deal of huffing and puffing and relearning each move. To avoid this stagnation, I encourage everyone to try and learn the entire Form on the other side.

You mean I should do the whole Form now on the other side?

Don't panic—I'm not expecting you to do it immediately. Once you feel competent performing the sequence as it is, go back and try the first posture in the Form, starting with the other leg and arm. It's actually not as difficult as you may think, and it will help break down the muscle memory rigidity that quickly sets in when we learn to perform an action with just one side of the body. It also has the benefit of liberating your mind to think about how else you can play with structure and order in Tai Chi.

I'd like to try, but not with the whole Form

In the Form I have taught you in this book, I have chosen specific postures that can be repeated easily on both sides of the body. Try it with *White Crane* and you will see how easy it actually is. Then try it with *Diagonal Flying*, or *Golden Rooster*. You'll see that it's not too difficult.

If you get stuck, just think about reversing whatever instinctively appears normal. So, for example, if you immediately begin to step forward with one leg, try the other leg. Let your own body figure out how to mirror.

Could I try this with a partner?

You certainly can. In fact, we often practice the mirroring exercise in class. Stand opposite your partner and, as she or he begins the Form, copy as though you were their mirrored reflection. For inspiration, take a look at the classic Groucho Marx mirror Scene and remember, it's not about working it out! Just go with the flow!

27

TRANSITIONS

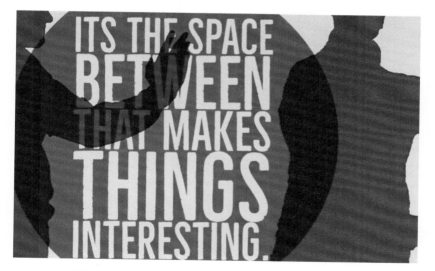

It is the space between that makes things interesting

Challenge 4: Exploring transitions: How to move smoothly from one side to another

Once you know how to mirror your Form, you can run through the whole thing on both sides. I'll explain below how to do this, but first I'll need to introduce the notion of a transition move.

What is a transition move?

Transitions have two meanings: they can either refer to the spaces between the moves in a Tai Chi Form, or they can refer to an additional posture inserted to connect two different moves.

A good Tai Chi player will incorporate these transitions seamlessly. To an observer, the Tai Chi moves are difficult to distinguish, as they appear to never end or start anew but rather fuse together into one long move that lasts from beginning to end.

A beginner may stop and start with each move as they explore the boundaries of the posture, but a competent player will rarely display anything other than continuous flow, and it is the transitions that permit this. It's similar to learning a language. At the beginning, each word you learn sounds distinct and clear, with a beginning and an end. But as you become more confident in a language, sentences form as an endless sequence of words, defined as much by context as by individual character.

As with the Tai Chi Form, each posture has a unique identity that is strong and well-defined for beginners to recognise when first learning, but as students progress, they find that the fusion between one move and another becomes as important as the moves themselves. The way you ultimately shift out of one move and into another can define the whole direction and purpose of the Form.

As you give more attention to these transitions, they will eventually create an identity that contributes to making the Form truly yours.

What transitional move can I add between performing the sequence on one side and then the other?

Choose anything you wish. The simplest transition is to step back out of *First Corner* so that your feet are parallel and shoulder-width apart, drop your arms to the sides, and then go straight into a move called *Shoulder Stroke* (see Chapter 29).

Transition from ending form - from Corner to Shoulder Stroke

From *Shoulder Stroke* you can easily return to the beginning again, and move straight into *White Crane* on the other side. However, do not feel you need to copy me; instead, feel free to adapt and create your own transition at this stage.

Take a look at the photos and check out the accompanying videos in the references section to see these examples in more detail.

And from Shoulder Stroke to White Crane .

NB: Want to see examples? Check out the online course for moving close-up examples.

28

REPETITIONS

GOLDEN ROOSTER

In the previous chapters, you have seen how to add a beginning and an end to your Form. There are two more ways we can add extra moves to the Form and we will be covering these in Challenges 5 and 6.

Challenge 5: Expanding your Form by adding extra repetitions

The first method is to repeat certain moves so that our Form begins to resemble the original Long Forms that used to be practiced. I mentioned earlier that some of the postures we have learned serve as excellent drills or partner exercises in themselves. These moves lend themselves to being repeated again and again, teaching us how to perform the move on both sides, working both the arms and the legs.

If you have worked through the challenge of mirroring your Form, then you will find this challenge easy. To start with, run through your normal sequence, but this time, try to add 3 repetitions of each to the following moves:

- *Step Back to Repulse Monkey*
- *Brush Knee and Push*
- *Step and Punch*
- *Diagonal Flying*
- *Golden Rooster*
- *Waving Hands*

If you add just 3 moves to each of the postures, you will end up on the same side as you began, and therefore can proceed as you were before. If you repeat a posture using even numbers, for example, x2, x4, or x6, then you will have effectively 'switched over' from the left to the right side, or vice versa.

What? Now I'm confused

Let's take *Golden Rooster* as an example. If you perform 3 of these (left, right, and then left again), then the following move, *Single Whip*, will continue with the left foot step back and left waist turn. But, were you to perform just 2 Roosters or 4, (left, right, left, right), then the step back would leave you on the other side, having to step back with your right foot and having to perform *Single Whip* in its **mirrored** position.

Of course, this could be an additional challenge should you wish, but I wouldn't advise it at this stage unless you are super confident with all the versions of the Form so far. Remember: for simplicity, add repetitions of odd numbers only. (3, 5, etc.)

NB: Want to see examples? Check out the online course for moving close-up examples.

29

THE EXTRA MOVES

The second way to extend your Form is to insert an extra move between the postures you have learned.

Isn't this just the transitions again?

Unlike the transitions that we looked at earlier that served to connect different postures together, these are complete Tai Chi postures in themselves and not merely adjustment steps or waist turns to accommodate a following move. If you wish to add extra moves to the Form—perhaps you have already done some Tai Chi and would like to add a favourite move from another style—then remember to only add moves that maintain the flow of the Form. For more on this subject, refer to Challenge 7 on **Rhythm and Flow**.

I've included a sample number of extra postures here. If you are familiar with any of these moves, you could try adding one or more of them:

- ***Shoulder Stroke***: Before moving into *White Crane*, a subtle extra turn of the shoulder, raising the left hand a little, and then a small weight change allows you to include this posture here as a transitional move between the Starting posture and *White Crane*. In both the Yang Short and Long Forms, *White Crane* emerges out of

Shoulder Stroke, so the two have a long history of flowing well together.

- **Withdraw**: *After completing Step and Punch and before entering Diagonal Flying.* Once again, this sequence appears in other Forms, and is often called *Withdraw and Push*, appearing in traditional Forms before the *Cross Hands* move. Although here we don't complete it in the traditional way, or follow up with *Cross Hands*, we can modify it to accommodate the next move of *Diagonal Flying*. Once the **Withdraw** has been completed, the hands shift away from what would have normally turned into a double push but instead become a "Passing palms" preparation for *Diagonal Flying*.

*After Step and Punch, you can add "Withdraw"
which leads into Diagonal Flying.*

- **Lifting Hands**: *After completing Golden Rooster and before beginning Single Whip, you can add Lifting Hands.* As you step back, the arms drop and then rise into the *Lifting Hands* position. Performing *Lifting Hands* here (before starting *Single Whip*) enables us to add an extra small spiral that helps push out the Hook hand on the turn as we begin *Single Whip*.

*Lifting Hands: From Rooster, step back, open
arms and bring to centre*

- ***Lotus Turn*** (**Optional Kick**): After completing *One Corner*, shift the weight into the back leg and turn in a circle, adding an optional *Lotus kick* here (see accompanying videos in the reference section) before ending your Form with the spiral hands and end position.

Lotus Kick is a fun, but quite complicated move

To get an idea of how these are practised, take a look at the resources section.

It requires a spinning turn, ending with a leg sweep. Watch the videos for a detailed breakdown.

Remember that these are just examples of extra moves. You can choose to add others that you think will go well with the sequence. Be creative!

After turning, flick out the left leg in an anti-clockwise circle. See video references of Form

So how many moves are there now in the Form?

These last two challenges can take your basic essential Form of 10 moves plus 2 (start and finish) and add another possible 16 moves, totalling 28. If you then mirror the whole sequence, you can end up with 56 or more moves. But numbers are not important, and please don't start calling the Form by the number you practise. Keep it flexible, keep it adaptable, and keep it yours. For a complete list of postures and the number of moves in each section and variation, take a look at the extra resources section.

NB: Want to see examples? Check out the online course for moving close-up examples.

30

RHYTHM AND FLOW

"A straight line may be the shortest distance between two points, but it is by no means the most interesting."

DR.WHO

Challenge 7: Search and find your own rhythm

Learning a Tai Chi Form by copying is a good start, but it's not our long-term aim. It can help us initially to get an idea of the shape and feel of the movement, but for the Form to truly come alive and become ours, we have to invest it with our own rhythm and flow. Otherwise, it will always remain a shadow of someone else's Form.

Make it yours by moving slow

If you watch a good Tai Chi practitioner, you'll see how they seem to move effortlessly between the moves. It's what some call flow. This **flow** is partly due to the reliance on using the tendon and ligament strength in and around the joints, rather than the big muscle groups of the body. This tensile strength builds gradually in a practitioner and enables them to maintain postures and move slowly but with incredible control. This slow-movement training is found in all aspects of Tai Chi practice.

Make it yours by finding the spirals and circles

In the Chen style of Tai Chi, you can see the practitioner's energy appear in the spirals and **silk-reeling** nature of the moves.

In the Yang styles, you'll see fewer spirals and more circles. Look at *Play Guitar, Waving Hands*, and many of the **Passing Palms** moves included within the framework of the Yang postures to get an idea.

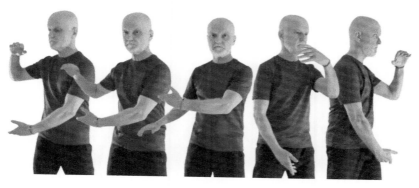

Waving Hands: to practice waist turns and passing palms

But the Yang style also offers another training aid that was introduced with the removal of the fast sections of the Form by Yang Chen Fu. By standardising the pace, Yang stylists have, over time, introduced another rhythm called Swing and Momentum. You'll find many moves that rely on this concept, such as *Brush knee, Step and Punch* and *Repulse Monkey* for example. Think of these as continual waves of energy with a repeatable and predictable rhythm.

Make it yours by employing the waist

The classic warm-up exercises of the waist turns are all training in Swing. Momentum is attained by employing the finish of an existing posture to gather sufficient energy to initiate the following one, almost in a kinetic way. As we turn and finish, let's say, *Diagonal Flying*, we utilise the waist turn to prepare the energy for *Waving Hands*. In this way, the entire Form can be seen as an ebb and flow, left and right, up and down, inwards and outwards. Play with the moves as you learn them; try and find this ebb and flow, and, as you build your tensile strength, you will find your Form will flow to a rhythm that is exclusively your own.

Flow is relaxing sufficiently that the arms can express what the waist creates.

Read the article on 6 techniques to develop your Flow

31

FINAL WORDS

Walking Your Own Path

As you can see, there are many ways to extend and contract your Form. My recommendation is to start with the basic 10 moves. Then, and only when you feel super confident with these, add a beginning and end. If, after this, you want more of a challenge, browse the list of challenges in this section and pick one that appeals to you.

Do I have the right to adapt or change a Form?

Remember, all Forms have adapted and changed over time and continue to be adapted today as each generation questions the relevance and utility of the practice. Some argue that this is wrong, but history shows us that this is a normal process in Tai Chi, as long as we adhere to the basic principles.

Finally, don't worry about what others say, just focus on your own practice. We all have a responsibility to continuously question and challenge the art so that it evolves and remains appropriate for the time and place in which it is practised.

Any final tips on change or adaption?

- Add moves that can be repeated easily. A clue is to look for postures that can be practised as separate drills, like *Waving Hands* or *Brush Knee*.
- Before adding a new move, ask yourself how easily it can be performed on either side.
- Check that adding a move contributes to the flow of the whole Form and does not disrupt it. Does your move

adhere to either a sense of spiralling energy or momentum and swing?

- Remember Lenin's prophecy that "the death throes of the old should become the birth pangs of the new." Consider this when reordering your postures and selecting what emerges from where.
- **The Classics** talk a lot about ups and downs, ins and outs, but also remember the left and right. Adopt an ambidextrous approach—balance your limbs, your directions, and your starting and ending paths—and you'll be on the right track.
- **KISS**: No, not each other—though that may be more helpful than the insults that often fly by. I mean, **Keep It Simple and Stupid**. Start easy, start gradually, and increase the challenge with each posture. For example, don't start with *Snake Creeps through Grass* (Google it) or even *Single Whip*; start with something easier like *Play Guitar* or *White Crane*.
- If you're teaching or demonstrating the Form to others, think more about what your students will be able to accomplish through your demonstrations than what you hope looks impressive.
- Remember that the Tai Chi Form is not the final frontier. Your mission is to explore strange new configurations, seek out new patterns and compositions, and boldly go where no one has gone before. (See references for the Audio podcast on this subject)

Finally

If you have any questions about any of this, drop me an email or contact me on social media, and I'll be happy to help out (if I possibly can). Look for my contact details in the About the Author section.

I hope this book inspires you to keep learning, keep practising, discover more about the art, and develop your own approach and ideas. And of course, share all that you learn—tell others what you've been doing and show them the moves too. If each one of us shares what we know with just one other person, then slowly but purposefully, we can all play a part in promoting Tai Chi across the world.

Remember, if you have received your code then you can join me in the video version of this book. You'll also find useful video links, book suggestions, and my extra training lists for you to print out and keep.

Enjoy your practice, and let me know how you get on.

SECTION VII: RESCOURCES

"The medium is the message."

MARSHALL MCLUHAN

32

LIST OF ALL POSTURE NAMES

A LIST OF ALL POSTURE NAMES

1. Opening
2. *Shoulder Stroke* on the Right
3. *White Crane*
4. *Repulse Monkey* (Repeated between 1-5 times)
5. *Play Guitar*
6. *Brush Knee* (Repeated between 1-5 times)
7. *Step, Deflect Down, and Punch* (Repeated between 1-5 times)
8. *Withdraw* (optional transitional move)
9. *Diagonal Flying* (Repeated between 1-5 times)
10. *Waving Hands* (Repeated between 1-5 times)
11. *Pummel fist* (optional transitional move)
12. *Golden Rooster* (Repeated between 1-5 times)
13. *Lift Hands*
14. *Single Whip*

15. *Cross Hands* (optional transitional move)
16. *First Corner* (Repeated between 1-4 times)
17. *Step Back to Turn the Wheel* - (transition move to left)
18. *Shoulder Stroke* on the left (optional transitional move)
19. *White Crane* on left
20. *Repulse Monkey* on left (Repeated between 1-5 times)
21. *Lift Hands* on left
22. *Brush Knee* on left (Repeated between 1-5 times)
23. *Step and Deflect* on left (Repeated between 1-5 times)
24. *Withdraw* on left (optional transitional move)
25. *Diagonal Flying* on left (Repeated between 1-5 times)
26. *Waving Hands* on left (Repeated between 1-5 times)
27. *Pummel Fist* on left (optional transitional move)
28. *Golden Rooster* on left (Repeated between 1-5 times)
29. *Lifting Hands* on left
30. Single Whip on left
31. *First Corner* on left (Repeated between 1-4 times)
32. *Lotus turn* (optional kick)
33. *Closure*

STEP FORM

If you chose not to do the online course that accompanies this book, then you can still see an example of this complete version, check out the Resource sections and the video of the **10 Step Tai Chi Form at Sunset.**

FOUR VARIATIONS ON THE BASIC FORM

1ST VERSION: 10 MOVES

1. *White Crane Spreads Its Wings*
2. *Step Back to Repulse the Monkey*
3. *Play Guitar*
4. Brush Knee and Push
5. *Step Forward, Deflect Downwards, Intercept and Punch*
6. *Diagonal Flying*
7. *Waving Hands in Clouds*
8. *Golden Rooster Stands on One Leg*
9. *Single Whip*
10. *First Corner*

This version is the easiest to teach, and from this you can adapt, work out the mirrors, the repetitions, and the transitional moves.

OPTIONAL 1ST VERSION WITH OPEN AND CLOSE ADDED: *12
MOVES TOTAL

*Starting Move (Extra)

1. *White Crane Spreads Its Wings*
2. *Step Back to Repulse the Monkey*
3. *Play Guitar*
4. *Brush Knee and Push*
5. *Step Forward, Deflect Downwards, Intercept and Punch*
6. *Diagonal Flying*
7. *Waving Hands in Clouds*
8. *Golden Rooster Stands on One Leg*
9. *Single Whip*
10. *First Corner*

*Close (Extra)

2ND VERSION: MIRRORED - 22 MOVES

Using the complete 1st version on both sides with opening and
close added.

*Starting Move

1. *White Crane Spreads Its Wings*
2. *Step Back to Repulse the Monkey*
3. *Play Guitar*
4. *Brush Knee and Push*
5. *Step Forward, Deflect Downwards, Intercept and Punch*

6. *Diagonal Flying*
7. *Waving Hands in Clouds*
8. *Golden Rooster Stands on One Leg (Right leg)*
9. *Single Whip*
10. *First Corner*

Transition, then repeat on the other side.

1. *White Crane Spreads Its Wings* (this time with right leg forward and left hand raised).
2. *Step Back to Repulse the Monkey* (turning left and steeping back with left leg)
3. *Play Guitar* (Right heel step etc)
4. *Brush Knee and Push*
5. *Step Forward, Deflect Downwards, Intercept and Punch*
6. *Diagonal Flying*
7. *Waving Hands in Clouds*
8. *Golden Rooster Stands on One Leg* (left leg)
9. *Single Whip* (turning to the right)
10. *First Corner*

*Close

3RD EXTENDED VERSION WITH SUGGESTED EXTRA MOVES*

1. *Starting Move*
2. *Shoulder Stroke*
3. *White Crane Spreads Its Wings*
4. *Step Back to Repulse the Monkey*

5. *Play Guitar*
6. *Brush Knee and Push*
7. *Step Forward, Deflect Downwards, Intercept and Punch*
8. **Withdraw with Passing Palms*
9. *Diagonal Flying*
10. *Waving Hands in Clouds*
11. *Golden Rooster Stands on One Leg*
12. *Single Whip*
13. *First Corner*
14. **Turn Body* (sweep Kick)

(Option to Repeat all postures on other side)

15.**Close*

4TH VERSION WITH EXTRA MOVES AND REPETITIONS ADDED

- *Starting Move*
- *Shoulder Stroke*
- *White Crane Spreads Its Wings*
- *Step Back to Repulse the Monkey* (x 3/5)
- *Play Guitar*
- *Brush Knee and Push* (x 3/5)
- *Step Forward, Deflect Downwards, Intercept and Punch* (x 3/5)
- *Withdraw with Passing Palms*
- *Diagonal Flying* (x 3/5)
- *Waving Hands in Clouds* (x 3/5)
- *Golden Rooster Stands on One Leg* (x 2)
- *Single Whip*

- *First Corner* (x 4)
- *Turn Body* (sweep Kick)

(If all repetitions are added, there is less need to repeat the whole Form as many of the postures will have been praised on both sides; however, it is good practice to do this set beginning on one side or the other to get an overall balance.)

- *Close*

Number of postures practised: Between 34 - 87.

And remember - take it all slow and easy. Work to your own rhythm and pace. Play, don't study.

34

ADDITIONAL RESOURCES

Non-course related video links and examples

Most of the resources can be found on either the training website or the articles website, and most videos are available on the teapot-monk YouTube channel. See About the Author for links.

Watch the form on the beach at dawn

This first link will take you to a cold morning sunrise on a South Devon beach in the UK.

This second link will take you to the training site. For members of the Tai Chi Academy (there is a free membership level), I organised a weekend online retreat for the 10 Step Form, which all members can access. The retreat explores ways to apply the principles outside the form.

A walk around some of the moves

I'm not sure how long this site will stay live, but while it does, you can make the most of the 360-degree views of many of the postures in the form.

Videos that redefine the way we look at Tai Chi (for the 21st century)

Many Tai Chi practitioners randomly quote Yang Chen Fu's 10 Principles of Tai Chi—though few will quote this musical, tongue-in-cheek version.

Ron Hogan: A reading from A Contemporary Take on the **Tao Te Ching.** If you have not seen Ron's version, try to get hold of a copy, as there are few other texts that relate this book to contemporary times.

Beginning and Ending: A rather relaxed, impromptu example of how to start and finish your Form.

The art of mirroring is a classic Tai Chi exercise with a partner in which you copy or emulate the actions of the other. For the ultimate example, consult the maestro: Groucho Marx

Another example of a Tai Chi exercise is called **Sticking** . It is an exercise that teaches how to communicate through a light touch, staying soft, and giving up control.

Repulse the Monkey explained: The slideshow that tries to put the Monkey Posture into context, though I should warn you, it does reveal more of the teapotmonk approach to Tai Chi than anything you will find in the **classics**.

More books

The Taoist book of wisdom from **Lao Tzu** has been interpreted by many writers over time, each with their own agenda. Students of Tai Chi may find this list helpful.

The **Classics** tend to be incorporated within other books on Tai Chi, but one book that dedicates itself exclusively is: *The Essence* *of T'ai Chi Ch'uan: The Literary Tradition* by Lo, Inn, Amacker, and Foe.

If you are a visual learner, you may feel drawn to exploring the graphical and interactive format in the **Illustrated Tai Chi Workbook**. It comes bundled with the Tai Chi for Health course.

Finally, for something very different, the application of Tai Chi ideas and principles to everyday living is explored in **The Manual of Bean Curd Boxing.** With Q&A sessions, colour illustrations, and contributions from Tarzan and a host of animals. Both books can be found at: https://taichi-store.com/

Articles & Courses

More articles on Tai Chi history including **Gifts for Gurus**, appear on my web site here (*https://www.teapotmonk.com/tai-chi-articles*)

Images

On **Instagram** you can find a number of Tai Chi related images and Infograms. Search for 21st century tai chi.

Audio

Talking Tai Chi with the teapotmonk podcast covers many aspects for both the beginner and advanced students. You can find it on Spotify or other podcast platforms.

35

THE ACCOMPANYING COURSE

Although this book stands alone as an instruction manual, I have attempted to provide further resources that will help your training.

- **The dedicated course:** This has been filmed, edited, and organised as a free complimentary resource for this book. If you have purchased this book from my book site, you will already have the access code.
- **Video References:** If you bought the book elsewhere, then you can make use of all the reference sections and QR codes in which examples and demos are given.
- **Longer forms**: If you wish to go on to learn a longer Form, then you may have noticed I have mentioned a few other postures and sequences (such as the *Embrace Tiger Return to Mountain* move in Cross Hands). These feature in longer versions of this form. Check what is on offer to you locally in Tai Chi classes, or if you prefer online options, I offer a 37 step form (Yang—Cheng Man-ch'ing tradition) as well as a 32 step Tai Chi sword form that are both open to complete beginners

If you need any additional help, contact me using the links over the page.

ABOUT THE AUTHOR

the teapotmonk

Paul Read was born in 1959 in London, United Kingdom.

As the unfulfilled '60s slid apologetically into the celebratory '70s, then lurched haphazardly into the divisive '80s, his itchy feet propelled him out of a Groundhog Day existence and abroad for the next 20 years. Now, with one foot in the UK and the other in Spain, he teaches, writes, and creates video courses. You may find him online as the *teapotmonk*.

Contact

teapotmonk@21stcenturytaichi.com

More Tai Chi :

- Articles - *www.teapotmonk.com*
- Training - *www.21stcenturytaichi.com*
- Books - *https://taichi-store.com*

ND - #0268 - 270125 - C0 - 210/148/12 - PB - 9781804676561 - Gloss Lamination